Praise for
Crossing the Tracks
for *Love*

Provocative, entertaining, and eye-opening. I wish I'd read this book when I began a cross-cultural relationship with a cowboy. It would have saved us much grief.

—Sara Davidson, author of *Cowboy* and *Loose Change*

As a psychotherapist, I deal with relationships for a living. Dr. Payne's work helped me understand the hidden rules many of my patients struggle with on a daily basis. It also prompted many funny conversations between my husband and me, such as about the time he took me to a Laundromat during our courtship. Having grown up in an upper-middle-class family, I had never been to one and was fascinated by it. He had grown up in a blue-collar family and had never known another way of washing his clothes!

—Dr. Jill Murray, author of *But I Love Him,
Destructive Relationships,* and *But He Never Hit Me*

Crossing the Tracks for Love *is groundbreaking. In it, Ruby Payne reveals essential keys for overcoming the hidden obstacles that cause conflict between people who truly love one another and are meant to be together. If a couple starts their relationship aware of this remarkable information, they can avoid years of unnecessary misunderstanding.*

—Donna LeBlanc, M.Ed., psychotherapist and
broadcaster, author of *The Passion Principle*

Other books by Ruby K. Payne, Ph.D.

A Framework for Understanding Poverty

Understanding Learning: The How, the Why, the What

Hidden Rules of Class at Work
(with Don Krabill)

What Every Church Member Should Know About Poverty
(with Rev. Bill Ehlig)

Bridges Out of Poverty: Strategies for Professionals and Communities
(with Philip DeVol and Terie Dreussi Smith)

Removing the Mask: Giftedness in Poverty
(with Paul Slocumb, Ed.D.)

Living on a Tightrope: A Survival Handbook for Principals
(with Bill Sommers, Ed.D.)

Crossing the Tracks for Love

what to do when you and your partner
grew up in different worlds

Ruby K. Payne, Ph.D.

aha!
Process,Inc.

Crossing the Tracks for Love: What to Do When You and Your Partner Grew Up in Different Worlds by Ruby K. Payne
© 2005 by aha! Process, Inc.

Copyediting by Dan Shenk
Book design by Sara Patton
Printed in the United States of America

ISBN 1-929229-33-x
Library of Congress Control Number: 2004111397

10 9 8 7 6 5 4 3 2

Contents

Acknowledgments

I would especially like to thank Stephanie Gunning for her writing. She completed the manuscript and made it so readable. I would also like to thank Peg Conrad and Dan Shenk for all their help and advice. Without these three individuals, this book would never have happened.

Many thanks to Frank, my former husband, and his mother and family for helping me understand the hidden rules of poverty and those of my own family of origin. Thanks also to our son, Tom, for being such an important part of the "story."

In addition, I would like to thank Arielle Ford, Ruth Weirich, Sara Patton, Kathi and Hobie Dunn at Dunn+Associates Design, Graham Van Dixhorn at Write to Your Market, Meg McAllister and Darcie Rowan of McAllister Communications, as well as the consultants and staff at aha! Process, Inc.

My deep appreciation extends to the individuals who agreed to be interviewed, and then so openly shared details from their childhoods, adult lives, and marriages. Your gift has made the book richer and more informative. Thank you.

Crossing the Tracks
for *Love*

Introduction

I'll never forget meeting the mother of my husband-to-be, Frank. She's a woman whom I dearly loved after we became better acquainted. At the time I was a 20-year-old student, waitressing my way through college by scrimping and saving my pennies. She looked me up and down and said, "Daddy's little rich girl, huh?" Those were the first words out of her mouth.

A heavyset woman with a formidable presence, "Mommy" was seated in a rocking chair on the front porch from which she could overlook the neighborhood. True enough, I was driving a Buick that belonged to my dad. But it was a big boat of a car, and nobody would have mistaken it for new. Her comment rendered me speechless.

When I didn't respond, she continued, "Where did you get those shoes?"

"Well, I bought them," I said. "They're Italian." I was proud of their stylishness.

"Those slacks! Where did you get those?"

"I made them," I replied. Back then I sewed all my clothes by hand.

Mommy only snorted at that: "Hmph."

After the tone of this introduction, I wondered, *Jeez Louise, what did I get myself into here?* Because I didn't know then that people in poverty often say something right off the bat to shock you and establish a power base, I felt as though she believed that I wasn't good enough to date her son. A moment later, as Frank and I were walking into the house, he said, "I would apologize, but it always looks this way." It was a mess inside. Pure chaos. It turns out Frank's mother was following a hidden rule of poverty: Before you can make a negative comment about me, I'm going to make a negative comment about you. She knew that if I were on the defensive, she would have the advantage.

Soon Mommy and I became friendly. I wasn't making much money on my waitress's salary, so I was living on one meal a day. When she found out, she kindly had Frank bring me over to her place for food. She also started taking me to rummage sales around town—or, rather, I drove her to the sales in my car. "What are you doing on Saturday, Ruby? Pick me up at 6 a.m." She always knew where the best garage sales and rummage sales around town would be. Church sales are the best ones, and you have to arrive early. We'd be standing by the entrance for half an hour, even if it was colder than Hades outside. We had to be first in line to get the best deals. Mommy was an ally of my subsequent marriage to her son, as well as serving as one of my earliest guides through the territory of poverty, about which I initially had no clue.

Frank and I are now divorced. But we were married for more than 30 years. He grew up in extreme poverty, and I grew up middle class. We met during college. For our marriage to survive as long as it did, we had to learn to understand and negotiate the differences arising from our economic backgrounds.

Frank's father died when he was six years old, and his family had to move. His widowed mother and her five children went from a middle-class neighborhood—and lifestyle—to a neighborhood full of generational poverty. Generational poverty is the phrase used to describe poverty in a family that's lasted more than two generations. Situational poverty, as in Frank's family, comes from a temporary reduction in resources due to a death, a divorce, or an illness. Many middle-class people experience this type of poverty during college or before they've established a career. Frank's family had to learn the underlying rules of their new neighborhood in order to blend in and survive.

As a person with a middle-class mindset, I was thoroughly confused when I met Frank's neighbors. Frank is a mix of Cherokee and Caucasian. The neighborhood was 98 percent white, with only a few

Hispanics and Native Americans, and almost no African Americans. I'd never seen people live as they did. Although they were making more money than I was, if they were paid on Friday, they were broke on Monday. Yet they hadn't paid their rent or made their car payments. I simply didn't understand the rules by which they were governing their lives.

Over the years, as I got to know his family (I found a gold mine in the stories and observations of his mother alone) and the many other players in "the neighborhood," I came to realize there are major differences between generational poverty and middle class — and that the biggest differences are not about money but about mindsets and behavior. For instance, Frank's friends were appalled that I didn't know how to fight physically. And I was absolutely appalled that they thought I should. I probably never would have thought anything about it until I saw the same differences among the students in the schools where I subsequently taught.

Typically, people don't think about the hidden rules by which they live. They simply live based on how they grew up. We don't usually learn about them — become conscious of them — until we accidentally break them.

Three or four months into my relationship with Frank, it became clear that my roommate had stolen our rent money. After getting a phone call from the landlord, I confronted her. She lied, telling me, "I paid it." Two days later, the landlord phoned again. So I called my roommate's father and asked, "Where's the money?" In middle class you're taught to use words to resolve conflicts. But she was livid. I couldn't figure it out. *Girl, you're the one who took the money.* I thought, *Why are you mad at me?* We had a conversation that escalated. She threatened to kill me.

Frank overheard part of the conversation and asked, "What's going on?" I explained. He said, "Did you talk to her?"

"Yes, but it didn't help."

"Did you *talk* to her?" he asked in a more menacing voice.

I said, "Gee, I thought I did." Clearly he meant something else.

So, he "talked" to my roommate on my behalf. Honestly, I don't know what he said. But she moved out the next day. And whenever she saw me after that, she would walk on the other side of the street.

Today, I understand that I broke a rule of poverty when I called my roommate's father. That rule is: Don't come straight out and tell parents about the things their child has done wrong. If you have to deliver bad news, do it through a story or in small increments, rather than point blank, such as: "Your daughter stole money."

A nice thing about being with a partner who operates according to different rules than yours is that you can step up for each other, as Frank did for me. When he saw my roommate basically pushing me around, he recognized me as defenseless within a certain set of social rules. He knew to "talk" to her because he knew how to speak her language. That situation gave me my first inkling that there was a whole bunch of stuff going on in Frank's environment that I didn't understand. It's also when I decided to learn the rules of his reality, which was now overlapping with mine.

What Are the Hidden Rules of Class?

Your best friend is seeing someone who is *so* dissimilar. You married someone who sees the world *so* differently from you. And that last fight you had . . . What was it *really* about? Could it have been about hidden rules of class?

Different environments create different rules. Hidden rules are the unspoken cuing mechanisms that people use to let you know that you do or do not belong. They make sense in a specific context. We have rules by race. We have them by religion. We have them by region of the country. We have them by economic class too. But we rarely talk about them.

How do you know that you've broken a hidden rule? Sometimes it's the way people look at you, which is basically the facial expression a person has after *seeing something moving in a wastebasket*. But even after you've just broken a hidden rule, people seldom say anything to you. You generally have to figure it out for yourself—or, if you're lucky, you have a mentor to walk you through the minefield.

Here's an example: A woman is being considered for an executive position. She and her husband are invited out to dinner. He isn't wearing a tie to a fashionable restaurant, and his table manners leave something to be desired. After the meal is over, the applicant and her husband leave. One executive looks at the other and says, "She married *him*? Forget her." The woman violated a hidden rule of wealth by having an inappropriately attired spouse whose social graces didn't measure up.

In short, *hidden rules represent mindsets, beliefs, and behaviors—and, indeed, there are hidden rules of class.* Hidden rules come out of poverty, middle class, and wealth because each of these environments requires different rules in order to survive and thrive.

A fascinating aspect of the 1990 movie *Pretty Woman*, starring Julia Roberts and Richard Gere, and the 2004 movie *The Notebook*, starring Ryan Gosling/James Garner and Rachel McAdams/Gena Rowlands, is the way in which both films' two main characters seek to bridge the considerable chasm between poverty and wealth (vaulting over middle class). Next time you watch these movies, think of them as studies in the complex, ironic, and often humorous nuances of the hidden rules of social classes—and how they clash.

Hidden rules exist throughout the world, of course, among all peoples and cultures, but this book's center of gravity is the United States of America. There are parallels, to be sure, between some of this nation's hidden rules and those of other countries and cultures, but there also are many differences. The exploration of those differences is beyond the scope of this book, which focuses on the U.S.

What put the whole picture of hidden rules into bas-relief for me were the six years that Frank and I, along with our son, Tom, spent in Illinois living among the wealthy. In 1986 we moved from Corpus Christi, Texas, to Chicago where my husband got a job as a bond trader for the Chicago Board of Trade. There we were rubbing elbows with people earning anywhere from $500,000 to $50 million a year. The addition of the third dimension, wealth, clarified the key differences between and among poverty, middle class, and wealth. I discovered that I didn't know the hidden rules of wealth any better than I'd known the rules of poverty. Furthermore, I learned that the wealthy look at the middle class in just about the same way that middle-class people look at those in poverty.

To show you my level of ignorance, when Frank came home from work one evening and mentioned, "Ruby, one of the traders' wives remodeled her kitchen and spent $18,000 on the countertop," I immediately asked, "Honey, how long was it?" I was looking at my own countertop, which cost $10 to $20 per linear foot, and quickly figured hers had to be about a third of a mile long. It never occurred to me that there was another way to think about a countertop. Frank laughed, saying, "It's shorter than yours."

I was confused. "Then I guess I just don't understand," I admitted.

"Ruby, it's pure Italian Carrara marble. Hand-cut."

On another occasion, the wife of a bond trader got sick, so (not knowing the hidden rules of wealth) I took her a casserole. Although that was a social *faux pas,* I didn't know it at the time. I even went upscale with a Pyrex bowl, which she didn't end up returning— breaking one of *my* hidden rules. When I got to her home, she took one look at my gift and said, "Put it in the *kitchen.*" Well, you know, I was upset that she was so rude. And she was irritated that I was so stupid. But nothing was ever said.

A big problem with hidden rules is that they're seldom articulated. But more importantly, they're equated with intelligence. You see, the first time you break a hidden rule, people say, "Ooh, I don't know about him/her." The second time, they just shake their heads. By the third time, they're telling their friends, "Well, you know, the wheel's turning, but the hamster's dead."

The problem is that hidden rules are learned. The group that has the most power, the most money, or the greatest number of people . . . they believe their own hidden rules are best. And, if you don't use them, they're sure it's because you're either rude or stupid. So the rules can drive a wedge between people who otherwise might get along.

When we lived in Illinois, I accepted a position as an elementary school principal in Barrington, a suburb you would not consider "poverty row." Ninety-five percent of my students' parents were in the country's top 1 percent of household incomes. As the principal of this affluent population, I began to rethink many of my beliefs about poverty and wealth. One of the myths we have in the U.S. is that if you're wealthy you're smarter. I believed I'd find that true. But when I got in there, I discovered I'd been hired because their achievement scores were low. The rich Illinois students had no more native intelligence than the poor students I'd worked with earlier in my career.

In addition, I noticed that the achievement levels of affluent African-American, Hispanic, and Asian children were similar to those of wealthy Caucasian children. If they had the same package of resources, there was absolutely no difference in their accomplishments. Money was not the only resource they needed.

In fact, researchers have identified ten fundamental resources that make students and adults good learners and highly functional. Several of these resources, such as emotional resilience, spirituality, and mental skills (reading, writing, and computing), are internal. Many of these resources, such as having role models, social support, and enough money, are external. Knowledge of hidden rules is an important internal resource. Even when individuals lack money, with other resources they can thrive and succeed. If they have money, yet lack other resources, they usually succumb to stress and falter.

The Origins of This Book

By the mid-1990s, after completing my doctoral dissertation at Loyola University of Chicago, I was back in the Texas educational system. I also was doing some reflecting on my learning about hidden rules and the three social classes in the United States. While serving as director of staff development in Baytown in the fall of 1994, an education colleague contacted me in desperation, saying, "Ruby, we've got 800 students, and last year we had 900 discipline referrals. My staff needs training. If we have another year like this one, I'm just not going to make it." Her building had been redistricted, going from 24 percent low-income to 64 percent low-income in two years.

"I need you to tell me more about your data," I answered. "I don't want to assign staff development unless we know a little bit more."

"Forget the data," she replied.

"Give me an example," I persisted.

"One thing that makes the teachers so mad is that the students laugh when they discipline them. And we've had many, many fights over the phrase 'your mama.' "

"Well, you've got to know that saying 'your mama' is partly cultural," I said matter-of-factly. "It's due to the role of the mother in poverty."

She went on: "We've also had many, many fights over 'he-said-she-said-you-said-they-said.' "

"Well," I said, "He-said-she-said fights usually involve an instigator, and if you know who the instigator is you can handle it."

Then the principal said, "Ruby, I don't understand. We give students a positive compliment and for the next two weeks they're the worst-behaved kids we've got."

"You don't want to do that positive stuff too much in public," I replied. "I mean, it's OK to do that with a group, but individually no. I'd do that privately. In public, people in poverty often will give a negative compliment."

She said, "I don't know what that is." One thing led to another, and she said, "You need to share this information with the teachers."

"They already know it, so it would only bore them," I answered.

"*I* had never heard it," she stated.

But I was convinced it was common knowledge. "It's in the research," I said.

Still the woman wouldn't take no for an answer. "Even if it is in the research," she said, "please come and share what you know." Finally, I relented. As a result, I spent five one-hour sessions after school with members of her staff. They found the material eye-opening, and they told other teachers they knew, who told others. By January 1995 I had lots of people calling me during the day from outside my district wanting information. Each phone call was basically an hour. It was putting me farther behind than normal. So I kept on saying, "Go read the research!"

One man called me back quite upset. He said, "I did a thorough search of the literature, and I can't find this type of information anywhere. Tell me where it is." In fact, I hadn't done a search myself. And when I did, I couldn't find it either. So I wrote a book for educators called *A Framework for Understanding Poverty*. The material for that and subsequent books — targeted to educators, churches, and social service agencies — comes from numerous sources. One in particular is my own marriage. In the intervening years, I've made more than a thousand presentations on this and related subjects.

An interesting phenomenon arose at my lectures and seminars. People in the audience began coming up to me on breaks and during mealtimes to let me know that the material on hidden rules rang true within their own close relationships and was influencing them for the better. They made such comments as:

- "This is the best marital seminar I've ever been to."

- "If I had known about the hidden rules sooner, I never would have divorced my first husband."

- "It's a huge relief to know that the disagreements my wife and I have aren't personally motivated."

- "Now that I understand the hidden rules, they don't seem like such a big deal."

Several people told me that they shared my information with their spouse and now feel empowered when they argue because they can agree: "Wow, that's really a hidden rule we're arguing about!" As a result, they take their conflicts to the level of the underlying issues instead of the personal level.

Since the volume of personal responses to the material was so impressive, I felt sure this was knowledge that could benefit many people. After all, statistics indicate that 40 percent of our nation's population shifts one economic class—up or down—within their lifetime. I decided to write a book where individuals and couples could turn to find pertinent facts and advice about coping with clashes between their hidden rules.

The Purpose of This Book

The book you're now holding explores the hidden rules of class as they show up in *relationships*—particularly marriage and other intimate relationships. It contains the kind of information I wish had been available when Frank and I were first married. My hope is that the insights of this short book will help you, the reader, be able to better understand—and perhaps reinterpret—your experiences in light of the *hidden rules* that each of us has inherited from our own original economic environments.

Each of us brings our personal hidden rules into our intimate relationships, whether we are dating or married. If you think about it, each of us is a rich piece of fabric that varies from person to person. We possess threads that come from our ethnicity, our race, our religion, and the region of the country in which we grew up. Then there are threads, such as gender, that cross cultures. Certain things are going to happen to you because you're a woman or a man, no matter where you live. Aging is another thread; things happen to you based on your age. Economics is another cross-cultural thread. There are patterns of poverty seen worldwide, whether you live in Haiti, Australia, or the U.S., that exist due to the cause-and-effect factors of daily survival.

Let me be clear. This book is about class, not race. Its purpose is to tease out this tiny, but significant, thread in our lives, which is economics, and make sense of how it affects our intimate relationships. There are many cultural differences that influence relationships too, and these are valid. I just don't feel qualified to discuss them.

I believe that every marriage and close relationship is unique, as are its two partners. Although we're talking about patterns in this book, I would be heartsick if the information were used to stereotype anyone. To discuss a group of people you must talk about their patterns of behavior, but if you start applying those patterns equally to everybody in a given group without regard to their individual personality, history, and preferences, you have stereotyped them. Please adopt an open-minded stance with respect to your partner and yourself—and others who are being described—as you try these ideas and patterns on for size.

Remember, I began my work on the hidden rules as a teacher and principal interested in helping students do better in school and to prepare them for successful lives. That meant showing young people how to make the transition out of poverty and function in the middle-class world of school and the workplace—*if* they chose to embrace those possibilities.

Similarly, I plan to teach you three sets of hidden rules (one for each economic class in the U.S.), so you know how and when to apply them. When we're making transitions from one class to another, or when we enter into relationships with people from backgrounds different from our own, it can be vitally important to understand that there are two sets of rules in operation underneath our interactions. This information helps reduce conflict.

There may be a time when you say, "I don't value that rule on my own, but I understand it and can live by it in this situation"—such as when you're dealing with your significant other's family and old friends, or when you're helping your spouse advance in his/her career by attending a business event or a meal with the boss and colleagues.

This book will not make value judgments about one set of rules over another set of rules. I'm not interested in changing your behavior or the behavior of your spouse or significant other. Indeed, I couldn't change you even if I wanted to. My only goal is to provide you with options—and awareness. When you know the hidden rules, you have more choices. You can choose whether or not you want to alter your behavior or embrace a different way of doing things. But unless you're informed, you won't get the opportunity to decide.

Code switching is the term social scientists use to describe the ability to follow different rules in different environments. Everyone already understands that there are different sets of rules for behavior. For instance, everyone knows you don't do the same things in a casino that you do in a church, right? Except praying, that is. If you learn the hidden rules, you can code switch as necessary.

The book is organized like peeling an onion—we'll go through layers and layers of issues that have to do with the different economic classes and their mindsets, habits, and guiding values. We'll examine the hidden rules of class that pertain to work, leisure time, gender identity, food, appearance, home furnishings, education, parenting, in-laws, money management, charity, social activities, and religion, among others. We'll also touch on communication styles and systems of conflict resolution.

In the process, it is my hope that we may all experience both illumination and healing in those relationships closest to our heart.

CHAPTER 1

Do You Understand the Hidden Rules of Class?

*L*et's start with a brief self-inventory. Please check the items that apply to you. There are no "right" or "wrong" answers, but if you have more than half of the items checked in a given section, it may tell you something about the nature of the relationship you have with your significant other.

Could You Cope with a Spouse/Partner Who Came from Generational Poverty (or Had That Mindset)?

It would bother me if my spouse or partner:

❑ Repeatedly gave money to a relative who would not work.

❑ Left household bills unpaid in order to give money to a relative.

❑ Loaned the car to a relative who doesn't have insurance and cannot be insured.

❑ Allowed a relative to move in and stay with you.

❑ Didn't pay attention to time (e.g., missed dates, was extremely late, didn't show).

❑ Quit jobs without having another one because he/she didn't like the boss.

❑ Cursed at his/her boss in public.

❑ Physically fought—fairly frequently.

❑ Didn't think education was important.

❑ Left items in the house unrepaired.

❑ Used physical punishment on the children as part of discipline.

❑ Viewed himself as a "fighter" or a "lover" who works hard physically.

❑ Served food from the stove, and ate most meals in front of the TV.

❑ Almost always had the TV and/or radio on, and often loudly.

❑ Kept the house dark on the inside—poorly lit and with window coverings closed.

❑ Kept organizational patterns of household chaotic.

❑ Bought clothing from secondhand stores, garage sales, and so on.

❑ Bought designer clothing or shoes for our children, but didn't pay an urgent household bill.

❑ Made a big deal about the quantity of food.

❑ Viewed me as a possession.

❑ Had family members who made fun of me for having a college degree.

❑ Bragged about me by talking badly about me.

❑ Chose to spend time with relatives, rather than spending time with me.

❑ Purchased alcoholic beverages for entertainment before paying for necessities (e.g., car insurance, utilities, rent).

Could You Cope with a Spouse/Partner Who Came from Middle Class (or Had That Mindset)?

It would bother me if my spouse or partner:

❑ Spent long hours at the office.

❑ Required our household to run on a budget.

❑ Planned out our week in advance.

❑ Started a college fund at the birth of our child.

❑ Hired a plumber to do a needed repair.

❑ Fixed the plumbing himself/herself.

❑ Played golf every weekend with his buddies.

❑ Kept a job that he/she hates for financial reasons.

❑ Rigidly adhered to time demands—and was often early.

❑ Was organized, keeping a paper trail on everything.

❑ Refused to give money to relatives who weren't working.

❑ Refused to allow a relative to come live with us.

❑ Planned vacations a year in advance.

❑ Spent evenings taking graduate courses.

❑ Devoted considerable time to a community charitable event.

❑ Shopped for high-quality clothing/shoes/accessories, then charged those items.

❑ Withdrew TV, computer, and other privileges from the children as part of discipline.

❑ Paid for our child's college expenses and tuition.

❑ Paid for tennis, golf, dance, swimming, and other types of lessons for our child.

❑ Often made a big issue over the quality of food.

❑ Bought reprints and numbered artwork as part of our home's décor.

❑ Purchased furniture for its practicality and match to the décor.

❑ Had family members who discounted me because of my lack of education or achievement.

Could You Cope with a Spouse/Partner Who Came from Old Money (or Had That Mindset)?

It would bother me if my spouse or partner:

❑ Spent money on private club memberships.

❑ Had a trust fund from birth.

❑ Insisted on the artistic quality and merit of household items, clothing, accessories, and so on.

❑ Had a personal assistant to assist with purchases of clothing and accessories.

❑ Spent money on a personal tailor and physical trainer.

❑ Spent a great deal of time on charitable activities and did not make or take money for that time.

❑ Placed our children in the care of a nanny.

❑ Insisted that our children be placed in private boarding schools at the age of six.

❑ Talked a lot about the presentation of food.

❑ Staffed and maintained homes in more than one country.

❑ Spent money on a private airplane and/or yacht.

- ❏ Established trust funds for our children at birth.

- ❏ Maintained social and financial connections with individuals whom I didn't like.

- ❏ Had family members who looked down on me because of my bloodline or pedigree (or lack thereof).

- ❏ Kept an accountant, lawyer, domestic service agency, and investment broker on retainer.

- ❏ Was adamant about details, insisting on perfection in virtually everything.

- ❏ Wanted to have nothing further to do with a decent individual who didn't have a suitable connection.

- ❏ Spent $1 million-plus on an original piece of art, and would *only* purchase original works of art.

- ❏ Attended an Ivy League college or university.

- ❏ Valued me largely for my social connections.

- ❏ Reviewed family assets and liabilities on a monthly basis.

- ❏ Purchased furniture and furnishings for their artistic merit or designer designation.

- ❏ Kept almost no food in the house.

Identifying what we cannot cope with or tolerate helps us to determine the hidden rules that we ourselves live by. If you placed a check mark next to several items in the poverty and middle-class mindset lists, most likely you are affluent or grew up in wealth. If you placed check marks next to items in the poverty and wealth mindset lists, you are probably middle class. And, if you placed most of your check marks beside items in the middle-class and wealthy mindset lists, chances are you grew up in poverty.

The Hidden Rules of Class and Relationships

When I was in San Francisco for a conference a few years ago, the man driving my limousine from the airport was a Russian immigrant. During the ride we conversed. In Russia he had been a teacher, and his wife had been a medical doctor, yet neither of them was practicing in the United States. I asked him whether he was glad he'd come to America, although he'd had to change professions, and he said yes. "Why?"

"It's a money pot," he said. "It's freedom." He told me that if you were a teacher right then in Russia, your average salary (if you were even getting paid) was equivalent to $25 a month. A loaf of bread cost about 68 cents. The driver went on to explain, "If you have to work all day long just to have enough money for food for one person for one day, that's what you're going to spend all your time doing. But if you can make enough money or food in one day to keep two people alive, that other person can do something besides survive and work."

The behavior of people from poverty, middle class, and wealth varies because the social classes have different degrees of economic freedom. Specific forms of behavior make sense in the context of having money or lacking money because people have a tendency to invent rules to help them adapt to their circumstances and fulfill their basic human needs. These rules circulate among family and friends, as success strategies get handed down. People also learn rules by emulating role models. In the end, the classes process information differently, and their decision making is driven by different forces. That's why mindsets, behavior, and beliefs are shared within groups. Everyone just knows this is the way "our kind of people" do things.

Over the years I have heard many people assert, "Money is important." Fair enough. Money is. But money doesn't change thinking. The research on lottery winners in the United States, for example, shows that within five years 80 to 90 percent are in worse financial shape than before they won. The majority of winners do not effectively modify their spending, saving, and investment habits to preserve their newfound wealth.

People tend to keep the same mindsets, the same habits, and the same belief systems that they've always had, even when they don't need them anymore to survive, unless two things happen: They enter a relationship, or they get an education.

Often couples make a mutual transition from poverty to middle class, or from middle class to wealth, when they find a way to increase their income. In other relationships one partner is climbing the income ladder. A marriage may initiate the transition, or people may meet and become a couple after the transition. No matter how they occur, transitional relationships put people in contact with unfamiliar mindsets and lifestyles. They can give folks access to more resources, as well as place greater stress on them. As the adage goes, "Everyone comes with baggage." That may be good, bad, or neutral. Multiple factors contribute to, or detract from, making a successful transition.

Even if you and your partner have the same financial standing today, it's possible that you're following two different sets of hidden rules, both originating in your childhoods. An "irritating" personality trait that you keep nagging your spouse to eliminate, or vice versa, may actually be a sign of a hidden rule. Would you recognize that rule —and understand it—if you saw it in action? Could you cope with the hidden rule in the long run if your spouse never renounced it? How harmonious your relationship ultimately can be depends on how well both you and your spouse are able to tolerate differences.

Is One Mindset Better Than Another?

One of the myths of middle class is that everybody (especially those in poverty) wants to be middle class. It isn't true. One of the myths of wealth is that everybody wants to be affluent. Also not true. What's true is that just about everybody wants more money, which is an altogether separate matter. Most people, however, haven't thought through the consequences of increased income.

Consider them now. Wouldn't you like to have $10 million a year? Think of all you could do with that money. *But* would you like to spend hours and hours with lawyers and accountants, making sure that you're not being ripped off; looking at legal agreements; planning debutante balls; dealing with dozens of requests a week for money from family, friends, strangers, charities, and other causes; and maybe even going to polo matches? You might want money, but you may not be too thrilled with the lifestyle and expectations that usually come with it.

Examine the middle-class lifestyle objectively. How desirable is it? Many middle-class people get up at 6 a.m. and scurry around before going to work. They work hard (eight to ten hours a day, sometimes more), then rush home to make dinner. They've got to take care of the laundry. They've got to go fill up the car with gas. I've been middle class, so I know very well. Just when they're exhausted, around 9 p.m., they might suddenly find out that one of their kids has a project due in school tomorrow. When this happened with my son, I ended up at Wal-Mart at 10 o'clock buying poster board, then stayed up half the night building the Great Wall of China. The next morning middle-class people get up, often in a state of sleep deprivation, and do it all over again.

One of the ladies in Frank's old neighborhood found out that I get up at 4 a.m. She was appalled. "Honey, you're crazy," she said. "You need to do like I do. I get up at 9 o'clock. I have a cup of coffee. I watch TV. Then I relax." Well, now who is the fool?

In middle class you also never quit a job until you have another one because you don't want to mess up your material security. Even if you're madder than a hornet, when you leave a job you write the company management a letter thanking them for the opportunity of working for them—you don't want to burn any bridges.

In generational poverty, when you get mad on the job, what do you do? You quit. And there are two things you do before you leave. You tell them what they can do with that job (and where they can put it), and you tell them what you think of them.

The daughter of a middle-class colleague of mine was dating a boy from an affluent family who decided he wanted to hold down a job for some pocket money. His father and grandfather were both on the board of directors of the bank. Although the teen had a trust fund, he wouldn't be able to access his personal wealth before age 21. So he got a job in a local factory. When his father found out where the boy was working, he came to the plant and demanded his son quit on the spot, saying, "There's never been a _____ who got a W-2 Form in his life. You will not work here."

Whether we come from poverty, middle class, or wealth, we think and act differently, as each environment or setting produces different strengths to ensure survival, along with its own set of hidden rules. Most workplaces in the United States today operate by middle-class values, and workers from poverty often find it difficult to learn or be successful. Too often, employers don't understand why an individual from poverty does not learn or respond as *they* would, even after repeated explanations. At the same time, workers don't understand what they're expected to produce and why.

Similar misunderstandings can happen in every area of life. Most schools, like workplaces, are structured according to middle-class values. If your spouse comes from poverty, you may have different interpretations about the importance of education both for yourself and for your children—or how to interact with your kids' teachers and school administrators. Without being prepared for what to expect in circumstances beyond our own experience, we all rely on the mindsets that made sense in the context of our original background. Your spouse may be surprised by what you take for granted.

Here's an example. Frank had four years of college and is an articulate man. Therefore, I was stunned by his response to a parent/teacher meeting at our son's school. Tom was in the third grade and had a problem with another child. Since I worked for the school district at the time, I said, "It would be better if you went up to the school because of my position." Little did I know what I had set up.

When Frank came home, he was livid. Almost verbatim, he said, "I will never go back up there again. They've got to go six-to-one to talk to you. They don't have the guts to talk to you one-on-one. They gang up on you." Well, he went to the school expecting to talk to one person, and the staff had brought in everyone involved in Tom's education, thinking, no doubt, that having everyone present would be the most efficient way of working at things. It also would show their commitment. When Frank saw six people waiting for him, as far as he was concerned, that was a fight. He made two of them cry before he left.

I could have been angry with Frank—I guess I was a little. However, I understood why he reacted as he did, and I have to admit that it made sense from his point of view. When he calmed down, we spoke about it and decided I'd be the primary one to handle parent/teacher meetings in the future. Either I'd attend them alone or we'd go together.

There are times when spouses from poverty will be better equipped to handle a certain kind of situation. On other occasions spouses from middle class and wealth will be better equipped. The context is the determining factor for who has the stronger ability to handle a particular problem or fulfill a specific need. Remember that many people want to expand their abilities. We aren't obliged to settle for the status quo.

Definitions of Poverty and Wealth

In the 2000 census the United States had 111 million households and 283 million people. Median household income—half having less and half having more—was around $44,000. To be considered "statistically rich" you had to be in the top 20 percent of households, those earning above $75,000 per year (with an overall average of $86,000). The lowest 20 percent had an annual income of $17,600 or less, which for a family of four was the official definition of poverty in 2001. Just 2 percent of households had an income above $200,000.

If you look at net worth (subtract liabilities from assets) in 2000, about 2 to 3 percent of households in the United States had a net worth of a million dollars or more. In the world there are 6 billion people. Only 1 billion people have an annual income of $7,500 or more in U.S. dollars.

Every race has its poor, its middle class, and its wealthy. The greatest numbers of people in poverty in the United States are Caucasian, because there are more Caucasians in our country than any other population. Statistically speaking, however, larger percentages of minority groups are poor. The highest percentage of poor appears to be Native American, followed by African Americans, Hispanics, Asians, and then Caucasians. Nationwide, childhood poverty runs around 20 percent, and it's growing in rural areas and first-ring suburbs.

Poverty exists for five main reasons:

- Lack of educational attainment.

- Family structure.

- Immigration.

- Language issues.

- Substance abuse and addiction; there are more biochemical problems in poverty than the other two classes due to the environment.

Women and children are at the greatest risk for poverty. In 1999 a woman needed to have educational achievement two levels higher than a man to earn equal pay. A woman with a bachelor's degree had a median income similar to a man with a high school diploma. A woman with a high school diploma had a median income similar to a man who had never gone to high school. Women with a high school degree or less are having the majority of children. One out of two marriages ends in divorce, and the kids tend to stay with the mother. Only about 30 percent of the people who are ordered to pay child support do. So mothers and their children often experience situational poverty.

Poverty is relative, and so is wealth. A lot of people comment, "We were poor growing up. But everybody was poor. We didn't think a thing about it." People who are wealthy often say, "It's all on paper anyhow." Or they'll cite someone who has more money than they do. So whether you're rich or poor is largely an internal measurement.

What Are Some of the Hidden Rules of Class?

When you're moving from poverty to middle class or from middle class to wealth, you're using part of the rules of the group with which you grew up and part of the rules of the group into which you're moving. However, if your family has been in any group for two generations or more, that group's hidden rules will be the only ones you know. These rules shape your thinking and behavior enormously.

If you were making the transition from welfare poverty to the working middle class, the poverty you could experience would be situational. Your values would include the importance of education. Middle class is the educational piece of the class puzzle. New-money wealth is about the level of your income and establishing a social network, though your other values may remain middle class. Old-money wealth is predominantly focused on maintaining and using connections to preserve wealth. The thinking, behavior, and values of each economic group are subtly different.

It's common in public schools to see students who have brand-new pair of Nikes or a Tommy Hilfiger shirt, but they can't pay for their books. Or students are on the free or reduced-cost lunch program, but they bring in a dollar or two every day for ice cream. Or they don't have a pencil and paper, but they've got the latest CDs and videos. Maybe there's a trailer court in your town where the mobile homes are beat up, but there's a brand-new satellite dish in the yard. These people operate by the hidden rules of money in poverty, which emphasize relationships with people and entertainment.

In middle class people typically meet their financial obligations first—meaning they make their house and car payments and take care of most of their other bills (except, perhaps, credit-card bills). Then, if they have a few bucks left, they might go to the movies. If you fall into this group, next time you get paid, try handling your money differently. Just once, go out and have a good time. Cash your paycheck at the local bar. Then, when the world gets clear and you can see again, check to see how much money you have left.

With the remaining money, pay the bills you can. Cycle off the bills you can't pay until the next payday.

I'm joking, yet when I make this suggestion to a roomful of hardworking teachers at my seminars, they've usually been middle class for so long they don't even find it funny. It offends their hidden rules.

Imagine if you were in that "entertainment comes first" poverty mindset for two generations or more. You would have few possessions. In rural poverty, families often have land, which means their outlook is basically middle class, though they don't have much cash. Why? You can't keep the land without the mindset of paying your bills before going out and having a good time. In the middle-class mindset of two generations or more, your decision making centers on three considerations: work, achievement, and material security.

In wealth that's existed for two generations or more, your thinking radically changes about money. You have so much money that you can't take care of it by yourself. You have to have people help you. A few years ago *Forbes* magazine published an article about a Brazilian construction tycoon with a personal fortune of a hundred million dollars. His investment counselor in Los Angeles squandered the Brazilian's entire fortune—and the Brazilian didn't know it for a month. If you're wealthy, your accountant can rip you off, your domestic staff knows all your habits and where your every possession is. If they wanted to rob or kidnap you, it would be easy. Therefore, you seek to ensure your security and your privacy, as well as to maintain your wealth. Your decision making is made against social, political, and financial considerations.

Table 1 on pages 26 and 27 compares (in shorthand) a handful of hidden rules among the classes that we'll be looking at in greater depth throughout this book. As you read them, please remember that these are general patterns rather than stereotypes. The mindsets and actions of different people in these groups may or may not conform to the patterns.

Table 1. Hidden Rules Among the Classes

	POVERTY
POSSESSIONS	People.
MONEY	To be used and spent.
PERSONALITY	Is for entertainment. Sense of humor highly valued.
SOCIAL EMPHASIS	Social inclusion of people he/she likes.
FOOD	Key question: Did you have enough? Quantity most important.
CLOTHING	Clothing valued for its individual style and expression of personality.
TIME	Present most important. Decisions made for "the moment," based on feelings or survival.
EDUCATION	Valued and revered in abstract but not as reality.
DESTINY	Believes in fate. Cannot do much to mitigate chance.
LANGUAGE	Casual register. Language is about survival.
FAMILY STRUCTURE	Tends to be matriarchal.
WORLDVIEW	Sees world in terms of local setting.
LOVE	Love and acceptance conditional, based on whether individual is liked.
DRIVING FORCES	Survival, relationships, entertainment.
HUMOR	About people, sex.

MIDDLE CLASS	WEALTH
Things.	One-of-a-kind objects, legacies, and pedigrees.
To be managed.	To be conserved and invested.
Is for acquisition and stability. Achievement highly valued.	Is for connections. Financial, political, social connections highly valued.
Emphasis on self-governance and self-sufficiency.	Emphasis on social exclusion.
Key question: Did you like it? Quality most important.	Key question: Was it presented well? Presentation most important.
Clothing valued for its quality and acceptance into norm of middle class. Label most important.	Clothing valued for its artistic sense and expression. Designer most important.
Future most important. Decisions made against future ramifications.	Traditions and history most important. Decisions made partially on basis of tradition and decorum.
Crucial for climbing ladder of success and making money.	Necessary tradition for making and maintaining connections.
Believes in choice. Can change future with good choices now.	Noblesse oblige.
Formal register. Language is about negotiation.	Formal register. Language is about networking.
Tends to be patriarchal.	Depends on who has money.
Sees world in terms of national setting.	Views world from international perspective.
Love and acceptance conditional, based largely on achievement.	Love and acceptance conditional, related to social standing and connections.
Work, achievement.	Financial, political, social connections.
About situations.	About social faux pas.

Understanding Is the First Step

Class clashes do not have to be disastrous. In fact, most are minor and can be used as opportunities to clear the air and improve communication. Your personal differences with your spouse or partner don't have to become an added source of tension in your relationship. Life itself provides plenty of challenges to overcome. Your relationship can survive as long as both individuals are resilient and remain committed to making it work.

Shifting thinking from the personal to the underlying is an important element in conflict resolution. While I cannot tell you exactly what to do to resolve any issues that arise in your relationship, if you understand what the real issues are that you're in conflict over, at least you'll know where to begin talking and what you need help with. Understanding the hidden rules is the first step in helping you and your mate make genuine decisions—and maintain both your partnership and the quality of mutual respect.

In the next chapter, before we delve deeper into ways that hidden rules show up in specific areas of life, we'll take a quick look at the qualities of resilient people. Then, as we explore the hidden rules together, it will make sense when I point out, "Here's an observable pattern, and here's an intervention you can use *if that pattern is causing friction in your relationship—or somehow getting in the way of your happiness and leading the life you want to lead.* Here's a pattern, and here's an intervention ... Here's another pattern, and here's another intervention ..."

CHAPTER 2

Ten Qualities of Resilient Relationships

*W*hat does it mean to be involved with or married to someone who comes from a different class background? Negotiation and a keen understanding of what is occurring are important. Knowledge of the hidden rules is important. Being able to talk about the hidden rules is even more crucial. These are healing mechanisms, so that if you want your relationship to continue, it *is* possible to have mutual respect most of the time.

Mutual respect is one of the keys to a long-lasting relationship. If there is any rule of thumb I have found in all my years of consulting with organizations and individuals on the hidden rules, it's that there must be an equal exchange, give and take, or resentment will occur on one or both sides. Someone who regularly gives and doesn't allow the other to give fosters resentment. Someone who habitually takes and rarely offers to give also is resented. What is given doesn't have to be the same, but it has to be recognized as valuable. For instance, one person may contribute money to the relationship, another person time. Intimate partners can offer each other companionship, supportive listening, affection, mentoring, and so forth, as well as gifts or financial support. Reciprocity is a demonstration of high esteem.

Marriages do best when both spouses are empowered. Personal power comes from different sources, such as money, education, and social connections. The greatest strength comes from the capacity to empower others—and that's a good way to measure success. It's important to know when to maintain power and when to relinquish it.

Another key issue in the survival of your relationship is the resources you bring with you into the relationship *and* the resources your significant other brings with him/her. Some resources are internal, others external. As elements in later chapters repeatedly demonstrate, the absence of various personal resources puts a strain on a couple. This lack increases the level of stress that you and your partner must manage, both individually and as a team. After all, relationships don't exist in a vacuum. Having many personal resources makes you a more resilient partner and strengthens your union. You and your significant other can draw upon each other's set of resources.

Ten Personal Resources of Resilient People

One of the questions I am asked frequently is: "Why do some people make it out of poverty and others don't?" The second question is: "That person has so much money, and he/she is so miserable. Why?" The third question I hear is: "We made an intervention to help someone, and it didn't work. Why not?" (Church people ask me this one a lot.)

Then I get a fourth comment, such as when an elderly gentleman in an audience came up to me and said, "Look, if I could make it out of poverty, *anybody* can!"

My response is universal. Making the transition out of poverty is based on the resources an individual has. Emotional well-being is dependent on resources too. There are ten personal resources, only one of which is money or access to money. In the case of that elderly gentleman, it turned out he had them all except for money. That made him extremely resilient, stable, and able to learn and adapt.

My son, Tom, had a friend in his late teens who came to live with us because he had nowhere else to go. When one looked at his resources, it wasn't hard to see why: Tom's friend has just two out of ten. Our family became his primary resource, and it's my hope that we served as a gateway experience, inspiring him to begin developing others. Much, of course, depended on him.

There are many factors in relationships, and these include personality issues. Where class overlaps with other factors is not an exact science. But my hope is that the following list of resources will shed a bit of light on the interventions that may be needed when you begin learning more about the hidden rules in your relationship. As you might imagine while perusing these items, a strong resource can compensate for a weak one.

The ten personal resources I have identified are:

- **Integrity:** *Integrity* is the extent to which there is congruence between someone's actions and a predictable moral and ethical code. In other words, people with high levels of *integrity* are consistent, honest, trustworthy, and loyal. They honor their promises. They take responsibility for themselves and don't need much or any supervision. They are accountable to others. They also are willing to step up and address tough issues head on.

Integrity is a major issue in a committed relationship—and also when you're dating. It can be difficult to negotiate relationship issues with a non-participating partner, or a partner who is deceitful or extremely impulsive. How one's partner acts and functions in the workplace also has a ripple effect at home. It shows a higher level of *integrity* if people maintain the legalities of their business. If a spouse becomes a liability on the job, there soon may be unemployment in the household or even criminal prosecution. *Integrity* involves self-discipline.

- **Financial resources:** This resource pertains not only to income levels, but also to spending, saving, and investment habits. People with a high level of *financial resources* have money, or access to money, when they need it, and they have the ability to plan ahead and control impulsivity. To successfully preserve wealth, a degree of knowledge about monetary systems is required (e.g., how to analyze a financial prospectus or portfolio of holdings, and how to use statistical data for decision making).

Many relationships crack under the pressure of economic conditions. As a colleague of mine recalls, "The toughest times we had together were when we were broke. It makes you tense. It's hard to kiss and act loving when you're stressed financially. Every past issue we've had has been around money. We look back on them all the time. For instance, when my husband ran a meat business for a while, there was a big struggle between us because I was the only one earning a consistent income. One week would be great for him, and one would be awful. It was difficult. We know a lot of couples that didn't make it through comparable circumstances. But fortunately we were strong enough."

■ **Emotional resources:** Research shows that *emotional resources* make the biggest difference in an individual's lifelong stability. The simple definition is that you have the ability to be alone when times are bad and not be destructive. If you don't have this capability, then you'll either get into destructive relationships or involve yourself in activities that are destructive, such as substance abuse. We all have tough times. The ability to make it through them is being able to hang in there and keep going anyhow.

Have you ever been angry with someone? When you were angry, did you think about doing bodily harm to that person? Were you ever mad at your boss, for instance? If the answer is yes (and be honest, it *is*), why didn't you walk into his/her office, reach across the desk, slap him/her, and say, "That won't happen again!" Your ability not to engage in destructive behaviors, such as these, helps you maintain a level of stability in your life.

Emotional resources also stem from relationships, another item listed below, so it factors into communication and negotiation. How do we ask for our needs to be met? How do we set boundaries? What do we say when we're happy, sad, angry, lonely, tired, or confused? Communication styles will be addressed at length in Chapter 16. For the purpose of introducing them in this current context, please understand that depending on the thrust of our communication, we use a Child voice, a Parent voice, or an Adult voice. The Child is resistant, rebellious, and needy—even whiny sometimes. The Parent can be negative and critical, or neutral and bossy. The Adult is rational, fair, and non-judgmental—a sign of healthier, less volatile relationships. When we speak in the Adult voice, we accord a listener the respect due to a peer, someone is who is neither above nor below us in status.

- **Mental resources:** Having *mental resources* at the most basic level means that you can read, write, and compute. It isn't a measure of native intelligence. It refers to the skill sets people need to function in the world at large. An important element of this factor is that it gives you the ability to know whether or not information you're receiving is correct. If you can't add and subtract, you can't really know how much of anything you have. I met a man in his mid-50s who is illiterate. He can't read or write. He can count to 20, but he can't compute. He sleeps with his wallet on him. It's a physical way to keep track of his money.

How well would you do grocery shopping if you couldn't read? You might look at the pictures on the boxes, but they don't always clearly depict the contents. What's on a box of dishwashing soap? Lemons. Not too long ago in Houston, an immigrant family bought some—thinking it was lemonade—mixed it with water and drank it. Family members ended up in the hospital. These are issues that come from not having *mental resources*. Of course, in this case it also was a language issue.

Interestingly, being able to communicate thoughts and feelings both orally and in writing is a vital *mental resource*. Understand that in every language there are five different spoken forms known as registers (see Chapter 16). Two of these registers are *casual* and *formal*. Casual register has a smaller vocabulary and contains fewer abstractions. Formal register is more articulate; it's the basis of communication in schools and workplaces. In relationships where partners have little or no formal register for describing abstractions and nuances, emotional disputes can easily lead to physical violence.

▪ **Spiritual resources:** Research on resiliency shows that one of the highest correlates with adults who make it out of difficult situations in childhood, then face tough times in adulthood, are their *spiritual resources.* Believing in a higher power, having a purpose for living, and making a contribution are huge factors in resiliency. These qualities bring hope.

According to studies done at Duke University's Center for the Study of Religion/Spirituality and Health, such results hold true across the board for all religions and faith traditions. It doesn't matter whether you're Christian, Jew, Buddhist, Muslim, or goddess worshipper, your resilience is increased by faith. This overlaps with *support systems,* due to attendance at religious services.

▪ **Physical resources:** Having *physical resources* means that your body works well (not that you own a car or other vehicle). Good health is the foundation of many activities. To be sure, chronic disability, illness, or pain can be managed, though they are personal stress factors. One partner serving as the other's caretaker also can put a severe strain on a marriage.

Let's look at *physical resources* as an example of how people need a full range of resources to be most resilient. A man in his 60s who has a serious disease could need medication and round-the-clock care—and feel depressed. If he lacks money but is able to do some positive self-talk, believes in God and a divine plan, and has access to *support systems,* he will probably do better than another person with the same disease, who, in addition to lacking money, also lacks an internal mechanism for processing his emotions, has no one to talk to or take care of him, and feels out of control and destined to suffer.

▪ **Support systems:** Which resource makes the biggest difference in success at work and in school? *Support systems.* And these don't only relate to money and friends. *Support systems* can be about having access to know-how.

Not having a *support system* in place means that you must spend more time on running a household, for instance, and coping with urgent matters that come up. It takes time away from being able to pursue learning and additional activities.

Middle-class folks have access to all kinds of know-how. They have access to *support systems* through insurance: life insurance, health insurance, car insurance, and so on. If they don't already know a doctor with a specialty they need, they have a friend who knows the doctor with the specialty. If they don't have a lawyer, they have an acquaintance who has a lawyer who can tell them whom to contact. They know how to get information. They know people to ask, and they can use the Internet. All of that is a support system.

Marriage can be a *support system,* and it can tie you into additional *support systems.* It can even tie you into a role model or models. Marriage also can tie you in knots, but that's another story!

▪ **Relationships and role models:** Research shows that having *relationships and role models* is the resource that makes the biggest difference in lifelong learning. In *The Growth of the Mind* (see Bibliography) Stanley I. Greenspan indicates that his research shows that very little learning occurs without a significant relationship. It should be pointed out, of course, that role models also can be destructive.

In my experience as a principal in an affluent community, I found that relationships are the resource some students did *not* have because their parents traveled a lot, had many social commitments, and worked very long hours. The irony is that it's the only item on the list that cannot be purchased. The Beatles were right in their song "Can't Buy Me Love": One cannot buy love and attention.

This resource is of utmost importance to anyone making the transition from one economic class to another. A consultant with my company describes a significant relationship that smoothed her transition.

> *My background is generational poverty, and my husband's is upper middle class. It has been quite an adjustment for him and his family. I might as well have been from another planet or country. At least when we first married I felt that way. Specifically, they were so stable and educated. They were gracious. My family was raw and uneducated. I didn't know how to fit in.*
>
> *There is no instruction manual on how to move out of poverty. Even though I had education, I had a lot of emotional baggage. One of my role models was my husband's mother. She is such a lady. I am grateful for her kindness, calmness, and putting things in perspective. She was always there for me. I could call her anytime, and she would be rational and help me problem-solve. She would never act critical of any of her children. She just helped them work through it. She thought in steps and planning, and she was very articulate. She helped me explain myself. One of the things we did together—since we both loved words—was have a "word of the day" that we would banter back and forth. Although we didn't live in the same town, we talked on the phone often.*
>
> *My mother-in-law played the role of the mother I never had. So she is my mother. By her role modeling, she taught me to be a much better mother to my own children. I was afraid to be a mother because I thought I might be like my mother, who, because she was manic-depressive, had highs and lows and was unpredictable. I didn't want to be that way. I have modeled a lot of my life on my mother-in-law.*

- ▪ **Knowledge of hidden rules:** By *"knowledge of hidden rules"* I mean being able to recognize and interpret the unspoken cues and habits of people in poverty, middle class, and wealth. In a relationship it's especially important to become aware of your own hidden rules, your partner's hidden rules, and those of any community in which you're circulating. If these remain unspoken and unconsidered, hidden from view, you may encounter disaster. Truly, this falls under the category of *support systems* because it promotes belonging.

What are your expectations for your significant other? What standards are you being asked to fulfill? Some relationships don't survive when a social cue is misunderstood. But if you discuss the rules ahead of time, you may prevent problems, such as the one in this true story.

A well-educated woman of my acquaintance from Minneapolis was dating an affluent man. One evening he took her to an exclusive private club that he frequented for drinks. Soon after they arrived, a man whom she had long wanted to meet walked into the room. She was excited and immediately got up, went over to the man's table and introduced herself. Audible gasping was heard throughout the room. When the woman returned to her own table, her companion was livid. He said, "I don't date table hoppers. Let's go!" They left the club, and he doesn't date her anymore.

Here's what happened. My acquaintance broke two hidden rules. She didn't understand that wealthy people always wait to be introduced, as a matter of security. The people who observed her *faux pas* had gasped because she was violating someone's privacy. Safety and privacy are two important reasons that exclusive establishments exist. Her date dropped her like a hot potato, as she had jeopardized his standing in the club. She had put his reliability in question because he brought someone who violated the rules. In fact, he went back later and apologized so he'd continue being allowed at the club.

Just as a couple might blend personality traits to be a stronger team—for example, an outgoing person helping a shyer spouse to socialize at an essential business function—you and your partner can blend your knowledge of hidden rules and other resources. In this case, if the woman had told her date of her desire to meet the man at the next table, perhaps using his social contacts, he could have arranged an introduction in a way they would have both enjoyed. They weren't yet acting as a team.

▪ **Desire and persistence:** *Desire* is the motivation that drives behavior. It's the impulse that gets us up in the morning when we'd rather sleep in. It's the energy that helps us overcome fear and surmount obstacles. When we want something strongly enough—when the outcome has enough meaning for us—we stick with it for the long term. You've surely heard the adage "A journey of a thousand miles begins with a single step." *Persistence* is walking and walking, day after day, making incremental steps of progress.

Without *desire,* there is no willingness. Without willpower or determination there is no persistence, no taking of action. Except in those rare instances when random good fortune smiles upon us, positive outcomes are the result of our own good efforts. So the tenth and final personal resource that we cultivate if we wish to be resilient is the type of *desire* that motivates *persistence.* This is the ability to link activity to meaning.

Will Your Relationship Survive? Assess Your Resources

Use the rubric (Table 2 on pages 40 to 43) first to assess your own resources, then the resources of your significant other. Be honest. With a highlighter or a pencil, mark the phrases in each category that best describe you, then your partner.

It's interesting to note that the number of resources a person has, along with the number of generations an individual has been in a particular class, greatly affects how pronounced his/her class patterns are. However, a rating of 0 doesn't necessarily imply a poverty mindset, nor does a rating of 4 necessarily imply a wealth mindset, except in the category of financial resources where that correlation is being directly measured.

This rating system is known as the Krabill/Payne Resource Quotient. It was designed for a research study reported in *Hidden Rules of Class at Work* (see Bibliography). Don Krabill and I found that the greater the number of resources an individual has, the greater his/her ability to make transitions and be successful in any environment. Whenever an individual gets down to 0 or 1 in several of the resource areas, that person needs a great deal of support from others.

So what are your resources? What are your partner's resources? Together with your significant other, do you have sufficient resources to weather the misunderstandings, the different hidden rules? Can you communicate about these issues and resolve the differences? Is the integrity there? Are you committed to a deep understanding of your partner and the culture in which he/she grew up? Having resources gives you a greater variety of options. If you and your spouse use the internal and external resources already present in your relationship, you may find ways to augment your other more deficient resources and thus to build a stronger, more resilient relationship.

We go through mutual experiences with people to whom we commit on a long-term basis—making a home, raising children, taking care of aging parents, running businesses, surviving tragedy, celebrating triumph—and many of these experiences put pressure on us. Relationships suffer when people are under stress, because then they're preoccupied with handling stress and not focused on developing their human potential and enjoying life's pleasures.

For a relationship to survive and improve, it's necessary for partners to understand their differences in a way that inspires mutual respect, embraces personal responsibility, allows for freedom of choice, creates increased cooperation and support, and includes opportunities for learning. Then the differences they have won't increase their burdens and cause rifts in the relationship.

Table 2. Krabill/Payne Resource Quotient

	0	1
INTEGRITY	Predictably amoral. Destructive to others. Practices deception.	Inconsistent. Unpredictable. No internal compass. Right and wrong are gray areas.
FINANCIAL	Bills unpaid. Creditors calling.	Paycheck to paycheck. Bills paid late.
EMOTIONAL	No emotional stamina. Impulsive. Engages in self-destructive behavior (addiction, violence, abusive adult relationships, casual sex).	Moves between voices of Child and Parent. Blames and accuses. Impulsive. Mood swings.
MENTAL	Relies totally on casual register and non-verbal data to communicate. Not much formal education. Disorganized.	Can read and write formal register. Prefers casual register. Can do basic math. Has difficulty managing time and tasks.
SPIRITUAL	Has no hope. Believes in fate. Choice and consequence are not linked. Discipline is about punishment, penance, forgiveness.	Believes in good and bad luck. Few choices are considered. Tries not to get caught.
PHYSICAL	Cannot take care of physical self. Requires assistance. Risky behaviors create health problems.	Can take care of self. Often sick. *Or* can take care of self but does not. Unkempt.

2	3	4
Consistently moral, ethical, legal. Decides in best interests of self. Rationalizes poor decisions.	Decisions are moral, ethical, legal. Avoids difficult issues. Is responsible for self but blames others.	Decisions are moral, ethical, legal. Tough issues are addressed. Accepts responsibility for self and is accountable to others.
More income than bills. Some savings.	Building assets in home. Limited investments.	Has net worth other than home. Many investments.
Uses Adult voice except in conflict. Outbursts of anger. Sometimes engages in impulsive behavior.	Uses Adult voice in conflict. Avoids conflict. Rarely impulsive.	Uses Adult voice in conflict. Confronts, yet maintains relationships. Is not impulsive.
Knows when to use formal register. Has some training beyond high school. Can implement a plan if told how. Knows the _what_, but not the _how_.	Uses formal register well. Formal education. Can do long-range planning. Knows the _what_ and the _how_.	Consistently uses formal register well. Knows the _what_, the _how_, _and_ the _why_. Initiates and executes plans. Has congruence between non-verbals and words.
Believes that choices affect destiny. Options are examined. Choices and consequences are linked. Believes in a higher power.	Believes that choices affect destiny. Is affiliated with spiritual, religious, or humanitarian group. Is self-governing. Believes in a higher power.	Thoughts and choices determine destiny. Actively participates in and supports humanitarian causes. Believes in a higher power and purpose larger than self.
Clean, presentable. Able to take care of self. Mostly healthy.	Attractive. Physically able. Mostly healthy.	Very attractive. Weight and height are proportional. Excellent physical health.

Table 2. Krabill/Payne Resource Quotient (continued)

	O	**1**
SUPPORT SYSTEMS	Alone.	Is providing support for limited group of people, which could include friends or family. Tries to build intimacy at work.
RELATIONSHIPS AND ROLE MODELS	Uncommitted relationships that are destructive or damaging.	Few bonding relationships of any kind. Perceives self as unlovable.
KNOWLEDGE OF HIDDEN RULES OF CLASS AT WORK	Knows and uses hidden rules of street at work.	Knows and uses hidden rules of hourly wages at work.
DESIRE AND PERSISTENCE	Low energy. Not motivated. Does not want to be promoted. Dislikes learning. Quits often.	Selective energy but maybe not at work. Works for the money. Does not seek promotion. Avoids training. Gives up easily.

2	3	4
Has support system of friends and family. Friends and family may not know appropriate hidden rules of individual's position.	Has support system at work and at home. Knows how to seek help if needed. Friends and family know appropriate hidden rules of individual's position.	Has support system at home, at work, in community. Has large network of professional colleagues. Can purchase help if needed.
Several personal relationships. Has several individuals who can be relied upon for help. Is loved.	Many personal and professional relationships. Is loved *and* has someone to love.	Large number of personal and professional relationships. Has been mentored and has mentored others.
Knows and uses hidden rules that members of middle management follow at work.	Knows and uses hidden rules that officials at executive level follow at work. Knows hidden rules of country club.	Knows and uses hidden rules that are followed in corporate boardroom and with charities. Understands organizational, social, business pedigree, and hierarchy.
Steady energy. Motivated by need to be personally right. Controls information. Wants to be promoted for the power. Attends training.	High energy. Motivated by need to be organizationally correct. Seeks out training. Promotion or rewards desired for recognition.	High energy. Motivated by challenge. Promotion or rewards reflect excellence. Constantly learning on his/her own. Very persistent.

CHAPTER 3

Driving Forces in Your Decision Making

*Y*ou have just received a call from your mother that your brother is in jail for "driving under the influence." She is crying and begs you to do something. You leave work, telling the boss you're going to go be with a sick child. This is the second time this week that you've left work for a family crisis. You take the rent money you've saved and go to the bail bondsman to get your brother out of jail. On the way home, because he's so depressed, you buy him a six-pack of beer.

You have just received a call from your mother that your brother is in jail for "driving under the influence." She is crying and begs you to do something. You calmly tell her that you cannot leave work and that your brother will have to wait until 6 o'clock that evening. You take some money out of your savings account to get him out of jail and tell him "this is it": You will not help him again. You then make arrangements for him to get professional help through his workplace's Employee Assistance Program.

You have just received a call from your mother that your brother is in jail for "driving under the influence." She is crying and begs you to do something. You call the family lawyer and have him post bail for your brother. The judge is a personal friend of yours. You arrange to have your brother checked into a detox facility, and he's given 100 hours of community service. You're particularly concerned about the publicity around this issue, so you have all of this arranged very discreetly.

Explanation

In generational poverty, decision making is driven primarily by survival, relationships, and entertainment. Entertainment is important because humor is the key tool to drive away the pain. The main possession you have is people, so relationships become all-important. You always have someone "at your back." Survival is the day-to-day reality.

In middle class, decision making is driven primarily by work, achievement, and material security. Middle-class people work hard at maintaining stability. You build material security by getting educated so that you have secure employment. This enables you to save money and build assets. Things are possessions. In middle class, if a relationship is significantly threatening your material security and employment, that relationship might have to be abandoned.

If you're from middle class and marry into poverty, you'll need to understand that things often don't carry the value they do in middle class. Tools are borrowed and not returned. The upkeep and maintenance necessary for property to be kept for years isn't understood. And the importance of lessons and education for the children is seldom understood.

In wealth, decision making is driven primarily by social, political, and financial considerations. Although material security is scarcely a factor in wealth, your personal safety becomes an issue. Without people around you serving as buffers, such as domestic staff, personal assistants, and bodyguards, you would be a vulnerable target for all kinds of approaches from people desiring access to your funds and influence—be they hostile or friendly. Not only do you connections keep you safe from physical jeopardy, they also protect you from intangible harm, such as loss of reputation. As we saw in the case of businesswoman Martha Stewart, the stock price of the company bearing her name plummeted after the 2004 legal verdict against her. It was bad for business.

The Role of Abundance and Scarcity

It is only human nature to seek predictability. People want to protect themselves in the future by learning from the past and the patterns it has revealed. Thus, our hidden rules of class are established. These are the different mindsets and beliefs guiding the behavior of people who variously grow up in poverty, middle class, and wealth. There is plenty of overlap between and among the classes in American culture. As we've already seen, people's financial situations often change dramatically, yet they still make decisions and navigate their lives according to the old, familiar rules—unless, that is, they enter into a relationship with someone who teaches them new rules . . . or they get an education. Their underlying mindsets influence decision making and are based on how they process information.

We cannot talk about the mindsets of the different economic classes without discussing the role of abundance and scarcity. *The fear of not having enough is very, very real in poverty* because it happens. Scarcity—the belief or feeling that there will never be enough— permeates people's thinking in poverty. This concept extends from money and income to every other area of life. Poverty is a fear-dominated reality that is less open-minded to new ideas because the external world is so unpredictable.

Here are two typical scenarios rooted in the poverty mindset of scarcity.

You go to the grocery store. You get your food stamps. You buy all the food you can until your money is gone. You eat well—steaks and ice cream—and you buy a lot of prepared food . . . but not many fruits or vegetables. The rest of the month you live off the awful food at the food bank. You also know how to go through the grocery store's garbage and find items that were thrown away by the expiration date.

Or you go to the grocery store. You buy lots of food because it looks good to eat. You already have a lot of food at the house. The refrigerator is full. But you buy more. You have back-up food in a bedroom. You have canned food that is three years old. You give away food, you make big meals, and you put the leftovers in the refrigerator. You don't throw away food when the expiration sticker says you should. Instead, you keep it and eat it.

When you make the transition from poverty to middle class, it's difficult to believe that there will be enough. That's why individuals

who grew up in poverty and move to middle class often become
pack rats. They won't throw anything away. Having "stuff" (food and
otherwise) is visible insurance that they'll never be without again,
and it's behavior based on fear.

To move to the concept of abundance, you must move away
from fear to trust. How can you do that if you've never experienced
abundance? The concept of abundance is that there will always be
enough, so in wealth, when the season is over, you give away clothing
that doesn't have significant artistic merit or historical value. You
leave your Armani at the cleaners. You have several anyway, and
you weren't particularly fond of that one. You redecorate the house,
giving away almost everything and starting over. You have a party
and buy dishes for the party because they go with the theme. When
the party is over, you donate the dishes to a charity. It's the concept
of abundance. What will jeopardize abundance in wealth are such
"intangibles" as war, national insecurity, falling stock prices, and
poor investment or legal advice.

Here's how you would likely behave when food shopping as an
affluent person. You rarely go to the grocery store. It is taken care of
by your domestic staff. If you do go, it's to a small outlet with gour-
met and select foods. You're very careful with your diet and rarely
buy food for the week ahead. Fruits, vegetables, meats, and seafood
are purchased and prepared fresh each day. Considerable time and
effort are given to the preparation of food, and only the finest spices
and oils are used. Calories are carefully counted. Very little food is
kept in the house. Frozen foods are rarely purchased.

Middle-class attitudes often lie somewhere between the two
concepts of abundance and scarcity. The big fear in middle class is
unemployment.

Here's how you would probably behave when food shopping as
a middle-class person. You go to the grocery store. You have a list of
groceries that you need. You have planned your meals for the week and
know what to buy. You have a budget that you're staying within,
and you're very careful about the nutritional aspects of the food.
When possible, you make food from "scratch," as it's less expensive

and more nutritious, but you will buy some mixes because they save time. You make sure that fruits and vegetables are part of the purchases, and you buy frozen foods that you store for a month or two.

In Chapter 5 we'll take a closer look at the hidden rules of class around food.

In *Your* Life ...

If you're from poverty and marry into middle class, expect that there will be little tolerance for wanting to keep everything and wearing clothes that have holes in them. In addition, money will be spent on items you consider unnecessary. For example, when Frank and I were buying a sofa I wanted a particular one because it matched the décor of our living room. "Come on, Ruby," he said. "That costs a thousand dollars! Over here is a couch that's $600 and it looks all right to me."

"Yeah," I replied, "but it's not the quality I want, and it doesn't fit the décor."

"But it doesn't have any holes in it!"

"My goodness! I should hope not."

The artistic presentation of the room was important to me. What was important to him was whether or not the couch was serviceable and economical. Why spend $1,000 on a couch when you can get a perfectly good one for $600? Who cares about the décor?

If you're from middle class and marry into poverty, expect that the fears around scarcity will show up on a regular basis. There will be too much food in the house. Items will be kept that should be thrown away. A friend of mine who came from extreme poverty and became a successful college professor still purchased all her clothes at Goodwill. Her middle-class husband would buy her lovely new clothes, but she wore the ones from Goodwill. Her husband would take her worn clothes to Goodwill. She would go and buy them back. She believed that it was frivolous and extravagant to wear anything else. Her reality of scarcity was such that she couldn't accept the better clothes.

If you're from middle class and marry into wealth, you'll need to address your tendency to be "wasteful and frivolous." Having lots of little knickknacks around is considered "cluttered and sentimental." When you redecorate, you won't have room for everything, so something has to go. Also, when you redecorate, you'll probably purchase things/furnishings that you don't like. They can't always be returned. So money will be spent on "mistakes." Items may be purchased for one-time use. You might buy clothes for one season. You might even buy clothes you never wear because, after you get them, you realize you don't like them—or the opportunity for the correct social occasion didn't occur as you had anticipated.

The Role of Perfection and Detail

You have moved into a new place, and the walls look awful. The landlord tells you that if you paint the apartment, he will provide the paint and deduct $50 from the rent for the first month. The paint is off-white. You paint with a roller and go about an inch away from the windows so that you don't get paint on them. Also, you don't use a drop cloth or plastic sheeting, and some of the paint gets on the carpet, which is old anyway. You try to rub it out with a wet cloth, but some of it stays, making the carpet brighter in some places than others. You finish in a couple of hours. When the landlord comes by to inspect your work, he's disgusted and claims you ruined his rug.

You have moved into a new place, and the walls need painting. The rental management representative says you can paint the apartment. However, if you get paint on the carpet, which is new, you will pay for the damages. You buy the paint, a drop cloth, brushes, masking tape, and a roller with a pan. You spend two hours taping everything before you begin. You cover the floor with two layers of plastic drop cloth, making sure the paint doesn't get on the carpet. You paint carefully, pull off the tape when you're finished, and check for any missed areas. You finish in a day. The rental management rep is pleased.

You have moved into a new place, and the walls are not the color you want. You hire a painter to paint the walls and carefully match the color samples to the fabric of the furniture you'll be using. You have the paint professionally mixed for the correct hue. Furthermore, you have selected three different shades and a special-effects type of look for one of the walls. The baseboard will be a slightly different shade. Additionally, the doors will be a bit darker and the crown molding yet a different shade. The painter is known for his painstaking attention to detail. He will even use a watercolor brush to get the finest edges. He tells you it will take at least three days or more to do the painting correctly because, in addition to the painting, he must prepare the walls. When he's finished, you inspect the room in detail. You are pleased.

Explanation

In poverty, details and perfection are not sought and rarely recognized. To pay attention to details in poverty is to be spoiled. ("What's the matter with you? Can't you be satisfied with what you have?") Because survival is the daily mantra, just getting it or getting it done is often the most important thing. So the details are immaterial.

In middle class, details are important, but perfection is not necessarily sought. Perfection tends to be equated with snobbery and likely comes at a cost (both in time and money) that middle-class people can't afford.

In wealth, perfection and details make or break you. One of the hidden rules that operate in wealth is that it's not OK not to be perfect. It would never be said that you must be perfect, but what is tacitly understood and rigidly adhered to is that perfection is expected. What is clearly understood in wealth is that a single element—one word in a legal agreement or one detail in a piece of furniture—can mean the assets go to someone else or distinguish a genuine antique from a reproduction.

Part of this perfection is a "class mask," which is how you wear your face. Emotional responses tend to be muted in wealth. The wealthy are taught for years not to show much emotional expression and to be very guarded—because if you have domestic help and you're watched all the time, you have to be careful. Also, if you're negotiating a multimillion-dollar business deal, you don't want to give away any of your trigger points.

People may say, "Rich people have ice water in their veins," but it isn't true. It's just that you're not going to give anyone much emotional response initially. To the other classes, this trait is disconcerting. But as they get to know affluent people, they can see that the feelings are there. They just aren't shown openly on the face.

In *Your* Life . . .

If you're from poverty and moving into middle class, understand that just getting the job done will not be enough. It must be done well, without obvious mistakes, and it must be cleaned up. Leaving a mess when you're finished will not be tolerated. It must be done with a high level of correctness.

If you're from middle class and marry into poverty, understand that doing projects may become a big area of frustration and contention. Agree on the ground rules before a project is started.

If you're from middle class and marry into wealth, expect that details and perfection will be a significant part of your life. Your partner will expect it. Regarding one couple I knew (he came from poverty, she came from wealth) . . . she demanded that he wipe out the sink with a paper towel after he got a drink so there would be no water spots. (And yes, they later got a divorce.) Over time, however, you may end up appreciating this attention to detail because it will save you in certain situations.

The Role of Planning

You're going to take some time off work. You don't know exactly what you're going to do, but you're going to relax. You'll take one day at a time and do what you want. You go out partying on Saturday night, the first day of your (unpaid) vacation from work. By Monday, you're broke. So you just stay at home and watch TV the rest of your days off.

You're going to take a vacation. You had to accommodate several different schedules to find a two-week block that would work for everyone. You filled out the paperwork six months ago to have the two weeks off. You'll be paid for both weeks, as vacation time is part of your benefits package. You and your family started researching and discussing the vacation six months ago. You made a list of places you wanted to go, a list of things to do, and a budget. Then you began eliminating options, finally settling on a place and activities your family could afford. You made the airline, hotel, and car reservations two months ago. You arranged for the dog to be at the kennel while you're gone and for the neighbor to bring in your mail.

You're going for a month to the beachfront property that you're leasing. You plan to fly on your corporate jet to the location. You make arrangements for key members of your domestic staff to fly in a few days ahead of time. Your personal requirements for food and the "toys" you'll be using are sent to the staff. Since this is a property you often frequent, you already have clothing there. In fact, you generally buy two or three of the same outfit and keep those same items of apparel at different locations.

Explanation

In poverty that has been in place for two generations or more, planning is rarely used and not understood. As day-to-day life is largely about survival, budgets for money or day planners to manage time are almost unheard of in poor households.

The ability to plan against a budget and a time frame is a key transition tool for survival in middle class. The budget is mostly about acquiring material security in this lifetime.

The ability to plan systematically—in multiple locations and with a replication of the situation from location to location—is a key transitional tool for survival in wealth. In addition, the budget in wealth is about sustainability over generations.

In *Your* Life . . .

If you're from poverty and move into middle class, learn how to use a day planner. It will be essential to your daily survival. In middle class, responsibility is defined as accountability to a task or a standard. To do that, one must have a method of keeping track of tasks. If a schedule book makes you feel "housebroken," then use a 3 × 5 note card, and every morning make a list of what you have to do that day. Put it in your pocket where it can't be seen, but where it can help you keep track of tasks and other details. Remember, many details involve relationships—and forgotten details often adversely affect relationships.

If you're from middle class and marry into poverty, understand that to be responsible for tasks is to invite being heavily relied on for help. Understand also that you'll be besieged with requests from individuals wanting you to help them get things done. Establish personal boundaries, then stick with them.

If you're from middle class and marry into wealth, understand that planning related to time and money will be a significant part of the relationship. Activities, social events, business meetings, and vacations are planned in advance—often months or even years ahead. Money is invested for two years and often more, as penalties are charged for changing your mind.

The Role of Destiny

In poverty there's a strong belief in fate and luck. The belief tends to be that you're simply fated or destined. So, in effect, there's very little you can do about who you are or what happens to you. Discipline tends to be about punishment and forgiveness: You were bad. I punish you. You are forgiven and, therefore, you have the right to do it again because *you cannot change who you are.* You can only be punished for it. Feeling fated also means you make many of your decisions impulsively. This is related to the whole issue of planning discussed above.

Here's a typical scenario. You get in the car, but you don't buckle your seatbelt. You hate that thing. It makes you feel tied up, confined. Your spouse/significant other reminds you that you need to buckle your seatbelt because it's the law. You say, "When it's my time to kick the bucket, it's my time. Leave me alone." When it's just you and the kids—and your spouse isn't with you—you don't make the children buckle up.

Here's a similar scenario with a middle-class slant. You get in the car. You buckle your seatbelt, and you don't start the car until everyone else is buckled up. Moreover, you make sure there are no heavy items in the car that could fly around should you be involved in an accident. Two years ago a major factor in your selection of the car was its safety rating.

In middle class there's a strong belief in choice—that is, I can control my destiny to a considerable degree if I make good choices. So discipline tends to be about choice and consequence: How can I make the choices that will give me the results I want?

In wealth there's a belief system called *noblesse oblige*—that is, "I was born to rule, and I need to be honorable about it. Therefore, I must be responsible for what happens." Discipline is about developing responsibility and controlling outcomes.

An affluent version of the scenario is: You get in the car and buckle your seatbelt. You have chosen a vehicle that has both front and side air bags, and you make certain the safety features in this car won't hurt you. You also had a special feature installed that sounds when another vehicle gets too close. This way everyone on the road is safer.

In *Your* Life . . .

If you're from poverty and marry into middle class, expect that individual behaviors will be held up against a set of behavioral standards. The personal idiosyncrasies and eccentricities that are allowed, laughed off, and forgiven in poverty usually aren't viewed as kindly by people from middle class.

If you're from middle class and marry into poverty, don't get caught up in a punishment/forgiveness cycle with your spouse, your spouse's family, or your children. Be very clear from the beginning of the relationship that responsibility for actions and decisions rests with the person who took or made them.

If you're from middle class and marry into wealth, understand the sense of obligation and responsibility that comes hand in glove with wealth. In affluence, a bad decision or mistake has a ripple effect on the lives of many employees. While not all individuals in wealth take their duties and responsibilities seriously, many do.

A Few More Mindsets

As you can see in the few scenarios we've visited in this chapter, there is interplay between personal resources and mindsets. People in poverty, middle class, and wealth make decisions using different criteria. By now, you've probably recognized elements of your behavior and/or your partner's behavior in these basic descriptions. While individual people's thought processes are influenced to a greater or lesser degree by such driving forces as scarcity/abundance, perfection and detail, planning, and destiny, there are a few additional factors worth considering.

In the next several chapters, as we continue looking at typical class scenarios and why they occur, we'll explore the following issues, which seem to surface as points of tension in many relationships. What commands our respect? What role is played in our lives by the senses? How do abstractions, paperwork, and record keeping influence different areas of our lives? Perhaps surprisingly, these factors show up again and again in the way we interact with our children and relatives, friends, and co-workers, the objects we surround ourselves with, how we spend our leisure time, and even who we perceive ourselves to be—our personal identity.

Happily, according to the anecdotes of the people I've spoken to, basic understanding and respect begin to reduce tensions and clashes between significant others.

CHAPTER 4

Your Gender Identity and Role as a Life Partner

Imagine that you're a single 47-year-old woman with a doctorate in anthropology. You're working in an area known for its poverty, doing an ethnographic study. You meet a man your age who has grown up in this area in extreme poverty—and there's an instantaneous spark between you. The two of you go out to get something to eat. A couple of his former girlfriends come up to the table and talk to him for five minutes. When the ex-girlfriends leave, he looks at you and says, "Why didn't you fight for me?"

You're a 47-year-old woman who has been married for 20 years. You meet a man who works at your workplace, and there's an immediate, mutual attraction. Like you, he's also married, and you both have children. The two of you discuss your attraction over coffee and decide simply to be friends.

You're a 47-year-old woman who has a substantial trust fund from new money. Your spouse/partner came from old money, but his trust fund was gone by the time you met. His connections are substantial, and together you make a handsome couple. He is on the boards of several charities and serves as a corporate diplomat. You periodically have a "boy toy," and he has a mistress, but each of you is discreet.

What's happening in each of these scenarios? Hidden rules of gender are at play.

Gender Identity and Class

It took me a long time to understand why the men in Frank's neighborhood would disappear. They'd be there for three or four months, and then they'd be gone. People were appearing and disappearing. One day, I asked, "What happened to so-and-so?" And I was told, "He's off visiting." I was so naïve that I said, "Did he quit his job to go visiting?" They laughed and called me funny, but they never explained.

Light was shed on the matter when I read an article in *Texas Monthly* 15 years ago explaining how a particular *barrio* in San Antonio got started during the Depression. Many of the men who lived in the community were without work. The authors of the piece quoted a sociologist who essentially said, If you want to break a culture, all you have to do is take away work from men, because it changes male identity.

We've been seeing the same thing happening in the Midwest for the past decade or two. A lot of small farmers are losing their farms. When men have work, they have an identity: They're a provider. When they lose the farm, their work is taken away. They become a part-time provider if they don't have the skills to get work in another business. Sometimes it gets so bad that even people with skills can't get work.

Being a part-time provider means there's no extra money to pursue hobbies. But if you have a mere dollar in your pocket, you can still get a cup of coffee downtown. Maybe you'll meet a nice woman in the coffee shop. The next thing you know, you're a lover. By the second generation of poverty, the two male identities that are most admired in generational poverty are physical "fighters" and "lovers."

Here's what I finally came to understand. When you're a physical fighter or a lover, you have to disappear for periods of time because people are looking for you. The law is usually seeking the fighters, and so is anyone they beat up. Let's say a man has been in a fight—possibly with good reason. He hears through the grapevine that the police are looking for him. He doesn't have bail money, so he runs and hides. He has to quit his job to do it. If he doesn't quit, they'll find him at his worksite. If he can cross state lines, he will. If he can't, he'll go to a different city. And if he can't do that, he'll go to somebody else's house to hide out.

After a couple of weeks, he'll be out of money. How is he going to stay alive unless someone gives him some money? His choices are to find a woman, get involved in criminal activity, or get a job. Of those three things, the easiest is to find another woman.

Everybody is looking for the lovers.

When people have work, they have role identity. We say, "I'm a teacher," "I'm a social worker," or, "I'm a stockbroker." Even marital references tend to be roles. We say, "I'm a spouse, a husband, a wife, a significant other, a fiancée, or a fiancé." But when you don't have work, all you have is your person, your gender. Your gender identity becomes "I'm a real man" or "I'm a real woman." Sexual activity is your proof of who you are.

Historically and archetypically, the gender roles for a male in U.S. culture have been those of "physical protector" and "provider." For females, the roles have been "caretaker" and "homemaker." This is true no matter what economic class they belong to. Most women have work in that they have children to look after. Work, however, is what enables a man to be a provider. When work is taken away from men, as it is during periods of high unemployment, the core of male identity often shifts to that of physical fighter or lover.

One of the things I've had to come to grips with in doing my research is that in poverty, sex is vitally important. Don't get me wrong. Sex is important to everybody—middle-class and wealthy people too. But it's not their only identity. If I ask a middle-class person who he or she is, he/she will probably respond by telling me what he/she does for a living. That's a role. An upper-class person describes familial and corporate connections. A role. In poverty, if you don't have work, all you have is your gender. It becomes a disproportionate factor in your overall identity. Unfortunately, whenever identity is largely established by sexual activity, it makes for an unsustainable condition. What happens as you age? You lose your sense of self.

To survive in poverty, because of the amount of violence, you must be able to physically fight. But to make the transition to middle class, the identity of physical fighter must be relinquished; otherwise you will gain a criminal record and/or experience periods of unemployment. Often, for a man making the transition from poverty to middle class, his identity will be "lover" and "provider." This is a blend of poverty and middle-class mindsets. It is possible to have a strong work history but not necessarily a strong relationship history.

Another reality in poverty: Your spouse or partner is a possession. They're *yours*. You physically fight for them. You prove to the world they are yours. And the rule is that they don't share their bodies with other people. For instance, it is not unusual that women don't want male doctors to examine their bodies. Husbands don't like doctors to see their wives' bodies either. At the end of her life, my mother-in-law was diabetic and refused to go to the doctor. Mommy was overweight and wouldn't take care of herself. This rule was so ingrained that she didn't go and didn't go, until Frank finally made her.

Still another characteristic behavior is that men typically socialize with men and women socialize with women. If a man is with a woman, the understanding is that it's a sexual relationship. The sexual relationship is usually male-dominant.

Finally, men and women in poverty tend to keep their money separate. The household is to be run from the money being managed by the woman. The male income is his to spend. A man frequently will give some money to his spouse/partner for the household, while he keeps a considerable portion for his own entertainment.

In middle class a spouse or partner is generally viewed as a companion. Couples go out to eat and do activities together. Usually both work outside the home, and financial decisions are made jointly as a couple. Often there are "yours," "mine," and "joint" bank accounts. Marriage is considered a partnership.

One woman describes this quality in her 25-year marriage.

We like each other a lot. We'd be good friends even if we weren't married. If you don't have a friend, the rest can't stand up under pressure. We have mutual respect, along with give and take. Within that sphere, there needs to be friendship and a genuine liking for the person. Otherwise it's hard to sustain the physical relationship. I like him. That makes a big difference.

My marriage has taught me tolerance for differences in people, because we're very different. Relationships need tolerance. There are days I don't like him as much, but tolerance is one of the tools that get you through. It's essential for those times when you're not looking at your partner through the eyes of awe and admiration.

Due to the advent of co-educational colleges and universities, and as a result of functioning as co-workers in business, middle-class men and women often also form friendships outside of marriage that don't involve sexual activity.

In wealth a spouse is part of one's social status. The woman is expected to bring beauty and an aesthetic sense to the household. How a spouse/partner looks, dresses, and so forth . . . are all important. (Physical expectations regarding appearance that are placed on women in wealth usually aren't placed to the same extent on men, although this seems to be changing.) Both spouses/partners play a social role as networkers and status symbols.

My cousin, who owns a $60 million company, told me an anecdote about a violation of the hidden rules of wealth. On this occasion, he asked a few of his managers to meet him at the country club. They were planning to conduct business with their spouses there to make it more pleasant, but one of the wives didn't fully understand. Before anyone else could handle the logistics, she stepped in and asked the hostess to put them right next to the piano bar. She was out of line. It wasn't her meeting. But once it was done, the others couldn't talk and be clearly heard. So she will never be invited again.

Some of the most vulnerable women I've met in my career were affluent women. Many lived on $200,000-plus a year and were well-educated. Despite having master's degrees, however, they'd never had professions. Their role was to have perfect children and to be perfect. Their husbands worked long hours—up to 16 hours a day —and the women's most important role was to enhance their men's social connections. They clearly understood what it would mean to lose their men. They'd live on $30,000 a year in alimony.

Bottom line: Women's vulnerability doesn't exist only in one economic class. But there is an added vulnerability among the affluent, unless they possess personal wealth. These women spend lots of time at the gym working on having perfect bodies. Looks are the ticket, at least until their mid-30s, at which time they're able to trade off their money and social connections. They have to provide clear value to the men in their lives.

What happens when a middle-class woman finds herself in this situation? A wealthy companion or spouse wants her to contribute social connections, so she'll foster friendships with prominent people by doing lots of volunteer work and activities. She'll take leadership positions at charitable organizations to establish her relationships. She'll work hard to ensure that she and her husband get the right tables at the right parties.

It's almost more important for someone in that position to learn the hidden rules than for anybody else. Wealthy women—and men —make or break their spouses at work. Once you get above middle management, you are linked to your spouse if you want to climb the executive ladder. So your spouse needs to carry the social ball.

There was a legal case in the U.S. in which a woman sued her ex-husband for additional assets because she said she made his career. He was worth about a $100 million. They were married for about 25 years, whereupon he divorced her and took a younger, "trophy" wife. His lawyers made a fuss about the fact that she had spent $20,000 on a dress, claiming she was extravagant. But she had to spend that much. Her clothes were expected to be designer-made and exceptional, and she had to have a new dress for every occasion. Her actual sin was that she gained 50 pounds. In her social circles, being overweight is taboo.

Chaotic Family Structures

There are two ways to be legally married in the United States: by common law and by license. At the time of this writing, to be common-law married in Texas (where I live), you have to meet three criteria:

- You must be together for at least one night, and you need proof. A child would be proof.

- There has to be evidence that you've commingled funds.

- You must have referenced each other in a spousal manner.

As you might imagine, it isn't difficult to meet these criteria.

In generational poverty there's a family structure that's not understood well by middle-class people. This is a single-parent household in which there are multiple common-law relationships. It took me 20 years to understand this structure. Here's an example.

In Frank's old neighborhood lives a woman we'll call Mona. She's white and in her late 50s. I've known her for 30 years. She married husband #1 when she was 17. I'm using the term "married" loosely. I believe it was common-law marriage because there was no formal divorce when they split up.

Mona married husband #2 when she was 19. This was a licensed marriage. With her second husband, she had a son, John. There was a lot of domestic violence in this situation, and eventually they split up. Husband #2 then entered a common-law relationship with a woman who also had been married before. They lived together for ten years before they got a license. Together they had a boy, John's half-brother.

Mona then married husband #3. Again it was a common-law arrangement. John's dad also has had at least two common-law arrangements over the years, as well as children by those women. In all, John has two half-siblings and four or five stepsiblings.

When John was 13, he fathered a child with a 13-year-old girl. They all came to live with Mona for a while. After a fight, the girl and the baby went to live with her grandmother, then her mother, and then the girl and her child moved in with another boy.

At 17, John dropped out of high school and entered into a relationship with a girl named Susan. Together they had a baby girl. By this time, Mona had left husband #3. She now began a relationship with Susan's *mother*.

If you were John and you didn't have an education, how would you describe these relationships? He calls his family members cousins, uncles, boyfriends, daddies, and sort-of-like-a-sister, sort-of-like-an-aunt. It's a confusing situation.

In sociological studies of human living arrangements, as well as animal populations, there's a common rule of thumb. The more non-blood layers you have moving in and out of a living arrangement, the greater the tendency for same-sex relationships to be adversarial —female to female and male to male.

Family structure is where we first learn how to handle the basic human dilemma of maintaining our individual freedom and yet living with a group of people. Most of us struggle with this dilemma to some degree every day. Family structure is where we learn our beginning concepts about cooperation, competition, authority, identity (particularly male identity), and deception.

In a culture of divorce and extended families, common law or otherwise, it's especially important to pay attention to the hidden rules of gender as they're acted out in different social classes. Gender identity, however it's defined, factors heavily into marriage and dating relationships.

In *Your* Life . . .

If you're from poverty and marry into middle class, understand that your spouse will have work and engage in professional relationships with members of the opposite sex. It doesn't mean they're going to bed together; it's the work environment that requires it. To be calling and checking up on your spouse, to make negative comments and accusations, will be met with disbelief and dismay.

If you're from middle class and marry or otherwise move into poverty, understand the need of your spouse/partner to protect you. You are his/her possession. Try to see the positives in this. Understand that jealousy will probably play a role in the relationship. Understand that deference is often given to men—and men are often "allowed" to engage in activities that are dangerous and outside the norm of legalities. Also understand that loyalty doesn't necessarily mean sexual loyalty ("boys will be boys," "men will be men"). However, your male partner will "have your back," that is, if you ever need help to survive, he'll be there for you.

If you're from middle class and marry into wealth, it will be important to note that the role of a woman in particular is different from her role in middle class. In old money it's usually considered demeaning for a wife to work for money, unless it's with a charitable foundation or an artistic endeavor. Rather she is to spend her time engaging in volunteer activities and making connections. The same kind of deference and indulgence that is given to men in poverty is given to women in wealth, with the exception of sexual license.

Not every relationship survives between men and women from different social classes. I know a middle-class guy who was dating an old-money girl. He couldn't pay for the bills at the private clubs to which she brought him. Her membership fees covered the expenses. But she wouldn't go anywhere else because that's where she felt comfortable and safe. He quit dating her because he couldn't pay for anything. When I asked him why, he said, "I'm not an equal player." There couldn't be mutual respect in their relationship because she was treating him as her "boy toy."

All of us tend to embrace the things we know. We're most comfortable with the familiar, so that's what we do. It's the same way in marriage. We use our families of origin as our marital role models. Sometimes this means we do the same as our parents, but sometimes it means we consciously strive to do the opposite.

During an interview, a colleague said:

My parents were children [mid-teens] when I was born, so they were still growing up and fought a lot. At one time, we lived in a chicken coop, and one time in a one-room house. We were in Oklahoma. Most of my childhood we lived in a one-car garage, a freestanding building on an alley at the back of a property. It had been converted into a three-room apartment with a live-in kitchen bedroom and half-bath. The kitchen was so narrow that an adult male could stand in the center and extend his arms and touch both walls. When they would argue, I had to go outside. Their fights would usually escalate into physical violence.

Already as a seven-year-old I decided I wanted out of poverty. My parents were fighting. I went outside where I sat and looked the stars and said aloud, "I'm getting out of this." From then on, to learn, I watched other people and saw that they did things differently. In high school, if I dated someone middle class, I soaked up everything I could about his life. I read. When I met my future husband, I was in college on scholarship. So we were peers, but I would say that he has always been my mentor all the years we've been married. There are so many ways I have learned from him. He wasn't critical; it's just that I observed him. I saw the respect that was there and embraced it.

When my husband and I married, we had several things in common. I was looking for a "perfect" family that I didn't have. He had a wonderful family and wanted to create the same kind of family he came from. So we were a good fit. Yes, I loved him. I was also smart enough to realize that if I dated men like my father, who was an alcoholic, I might marry them. It sounds calculating, but my goal was not to be in the same situation I'd been in. That was an emotional resource: standing outside myself and analyzing any situation I happened to be in. I never dated anyone who didn't have the values and family training that I thought would support my vision.

In addition, we both wanted to be in the marriage for the long haul, which doesn't mean it couldn't have broken apart, but he was the strong-glue partner. That comes from his personality and upbringing. He was a mentor to me.

CHAPTER 5

Food as Love, Food as Art

Food—its preparation, how it is served, and its quantity and quality—is an important beginning indicator of the hidden rules of class for many people. Food is emblematic of abundance, as the contrasting scenarios about grocery shopping in Chapter 3 demonstrated.

In generational poverty, the *quantity* of food is very important. Questions people might ask after a meal include: "Are you full?" and "Did you have enough?" In poverty, a disproportionate amount of income goes to food. Part of the reason for that is that the incomes are less. But another part of the reason for that is that food represents the line between being destitute and merely being poor. To run out of food or to eat very little is considered insulting. Having plenty of food is evidence that you aren't destitute.

A trainer at my company, who successfully made the transition out of poverty with her husband in the early years of their marriage, showed him the three checklists in Chapter 1. Afterward she told me, "He doesn't consider himself 'from poverty.' But there was situational poverty. It depended on his dad's job situation. There were times the family got down to a bag of potatoes. He just won't admit it." In my work, people often say to me, "Ruby, we were poor growing up, but we always had enough to eat."

Recent news reports have cited the amount of obesity in poverty. What is not understood in the news is the mindset of poverty. Food in poverty is equated with love and forgiveness. So if you want to show people that you love them, you get them food. If you are well-fed, the inference is that you are well-loved. You may even have the "love handles" to prove it. People who grew up poor—and who now have considerably more money—still tend to keep lots of food in the house. The pantry is full.

"My husband was one of five children. To feed seven mouths, his father planted a garden and grew vegetables," reported a woman in a 24-year marriage, who says her parents raised her to maintain middle-class rules without the money. "Although I was the primary cook when our kids were little, he loves to cook and prepares most meals now. When I come home after being on the road, there's always something in the kitchen that's my favorite. I do the baking of sweets like cakes. But he'll always put orange sherbet in the freezer. Typically he never says anything about it. In his mind, he's picked up something that I like to please me. Food—not flowers—is love for him.

"Food is a source of entertainment in our household," the woman continued. "In my family, when we get together, the first thing we do is discuss, 'What are we going to fix?' That's what it's like. Both kids are in college now. I love thinking of what to feed them when they come home. I don't ask them 'What do you want to do?' I ask them 'What do you want to eat?' I've never gone to bed hungry. I eat when I'm happy, sad, mad, glad, or just don't care."

In middle class there's enough food. People often are on a diet. The main issue around food is its quality, and typical questions after a meal might be: "Did you like it?" "Was it good?" and "How did it taste?" Food is purchased as needed to replace household staples or to prepare a special meal.

A middle-class acquaintance describes food as one of the two main areas of conflict in during her marriage.

> It seems trivial now, but I can remember that food was once a big issue. My husband and I had to accommodate differences about money and food. He was one of 12 siblings, so in his family the issue was: "Is everyone fed? Have we taken care of the hunger?" To this day, it's very important to him. "Did you have enough?" Quantity was never an issue in my family. What we care about is: "How did everything taste?"

> *When our children were little, my husband would make big pots of food to eat, but the kids wouldn't eat what he made. They wanted pretty, tasty food, so they refused. "You don't understand," he would say. "You should eat it." But I wouldn't let him push it onto them. "I don't blame them," I would say.*
>
> *Ultimately, we compromised. I'd remind him, "You don't need to fix so much. Put a salad with it." And I'd educate him by asking, "What goes with that?" His usual response was, "I never thought much about it." I don't cook much, so it's his thing. Even though I don't really like to cook, he allows me to make suggestions.*

Among the wealthy, the central issue around food is its presentation. Common questions after a meal are: "Was it well presented? Did it have aesthetic appeal? Did it go well with the theme of the event?" In wealth, little food is kept in the house. Food is purchased for an event or a meal, but food isn't equated with love.

As Babe Paley, an icon of glamour and style in the mid-20th century, once said, "One can never be too thin or too rich." To be thin is to be in. Because the camera adds ten pounds to any picture, to be underweight is to look better in photos. Because artistic merit is so important in wealth, the body is greatly valued for its appearance. So among the wealthy, to be thin is desirable—and it's tacitly understood that being overweight is *not* desirable. (This mindset has crossed over into the popular culture, affecting middle class as well.) *Haute couture* designers simply will not design clothing above a size 14 for women.

Contrasting Scenarios

You finally meet the family. It's Thanksgiving dinner. It's loud and chaotic, and there's nearly a fistfight. The table isn't set, and there is little room on it for food, as it's overflowing with papers, bills, open bags of chips, and so on. Family members grab paper plates and fill them straight from the stove. They wander in over a two-hour period to eat. People eat while watching the football game on TV. Everyone talks at the same time.

You finally meet the family. It's Thanksgiving dinner. The table is set. Everyone brings a side dish for the dinner, which begins at 1 p.m. The entire family is there, seated at the table. The dinner begins with a blessing. Food is served in dishes and passed around. When one person talks, others listen—at least most of the time. Children who interrupt may be reminded not to.

You finally meet the family. It's Thanksgiving dinner. The table is set. Cocktails begin at 7 p.m. Dinner will be served at 8. Guests dress for dinner. Dinner is served either by household staff or a caterer. Conversation is mixed. Sometimes you speak one on one with the person next to you, sometimes everyone speaks as a group, each listening to the other. Name placeholders are used to designate seating.

In *Your* Life ...

If you come from a middle-class background and marry into wealth, food preparation, food presentation, and adherence to a theme are *very* important skills to develop. Learn about extended silverware and silver settings and the different pieces of crystal used to drink different beverages—and take cooking classes. Never, but *never,* make fun of yourself as a deficient cook. Be extremely knowledgeable about wine. This is essential. Even if you don't personally imbibe alcohol, you'll be required to serve it.

A friend of mine is a chef who gives classes to wealthy women on cooking Thai food (he lived in Thailand for many years). He tells the story of a "trophy" wife who came to cooking classes with her husband. Midway through the first class, the woman stood up and said to her husband, "I'm leaving. This is why we have the maid." Both walked out. When they were out of earshot, one of the older wealthy women in attendance said quietly, but loudly enough so that everyone in the room could hear, "Retread."

By sarcastically equating the woman who walked out to the new-looking cover put on an old, bald tire, this critic was not only commenting on the woman's social *faux pas* but also on the man's poor taste in marrying her and the nature of their relationship.

Another friend of mine tells a story of a dinner party where the middle-class hostess served white rice with paella. As she said, "We laughed about that for days!" In short, white rice is *never* served with authentic paella.

If you are moving from poverty into middle class, it's important to learn how to set a table properly and how to decorate it for holidays. Food is to be served in dishes and not off the stove. The table is to be set before anyone is seated.

If you grew up middle class and marry into poverty, understand the issue with food and love. Don't serve alcoholic beverages at extended-family dinners unless you want to increase the likelihood of a physical fight. The kitchen is generally the family meeting place. Women are expected to cook, and men expect to be served.

CHAPTER 6

Your Appearance Tells a Tale

magine you're going to a wedding. You and your spouse/partner are best man and matron of honor. The wedding is held on the front porch of a friend's house. The groom is wearing a dress shirt, blue jeans, and boots. The bride has on a sequined, full-length dress. Your partner/spouse puts on a pair of clean blue jeans, a T-shirt, and a baseball-type cap. You are wearing a dress and sandals. The wedding is officiated by the Justice of the Peace. Afterward, there's a big party in the backyard. Beer is provided in kegs, and friends who want hard liquor bring their own. You get a sheet cake from the grocery store. Hamburgers and hot dogs are the order of the day.

You're going to a wedding. You and your spouse/partner are best man and matron of honor. The wedding is at a church. The men wear rented tuxes, and the women have on matching dresses. Invitations were sent out a couple of months in advance. The bride and wedding party have fresh flowers. The wedding is followed by a reception at the church, where a deejay plays recorded music and good-natured stories are told about the bride and groom. There's a buffet and a tiered cake for dessert.

You're going to a wedding. You and your spouse/partner are best man and matron of honor. The wedding is in a cathedral. Tuxes are tailor-made, and the bride's gown and the gowns of her bridal party are designer originals. The reception is catered at a local hotel where an entire floor, including a ballroom, is reserved for the wedding party and guests. Music is live. An invitation is required for entry. Security guards are everywhere, but their presence is discreet. In tuxes and suits, they appear to be guests.

Explanation

In generational poverty, appearance is either ignored *or* admired for its personal style and idiosyncratic statement. In other words, when you don't have money, all you have is personal style. Clothes are proof of someone's love or of being special. Personality is displayed through the clothes. Parents often will purchase designer clothes or designer shoes for their children. These constitute proof that they made a sacrifice for their kids and that they love them. Adolescents will "kill" for a designer jacket or shoes. Makeup is heavily applied or nonexistent. Hair is over-processed or scarcely addressed. Accessories (jewelry) tend to be gaudy.

In middle class, clothing is about status. This is true for both men and women. Clothing is chosen for its quality, its brand name, and whether it can be afforded. Workmanship is mediocre, and fit is not the primary concern. Expensive fabrics are avoided because of the cost of cleaning and maintenance. Clothing is often selected to be representative of your career position and indicates your taste and knowledge of appropriateness. Men who work in corporate offices, for instance, wear suits and ties. In other places of business, the dress code may be more sporty and casual.

Women's makeup is heavier in the middle class than in wealth, and it's often noticeable. The same makeup tends to be used day after day and is changed only with the purchase of some new cosmetic item. Hair in middle class is a decent cut. You wear the best jewelry you have; there are some good gold pieces and lots of sterling silver. Watches run in the $50 to $500 range. Clothing is color-coordinated. Shoes can be trendy, but basic shoes for work are kept two or three years.

In wealth, women's clothing is chosen for artistic and aesthetic reasons. One's body is expected to make an artistic statement, and clothing assists in achieving that objective. Jewelry is minimal and, again, chosen for the understated fashion statement it will make. The quality of your haircut is important. Being fit is *very* important. For men, there's more latitude in what is acceptable, but a man must be keenly aware of the setting in which he's operating. A fashion *faux pas* can be every bit as injurious to a wealthy man's career and standing in the community as to a woman's.

In wealth, women use makeup to enhance their features and carefully choose it for an exact shade and effect. Makeup is light and almost imperceptible. Eye shadow is also lightly applied and isn't obvious. It's not unusual that, prior to a social gathering, makeup will be applied professionally to match a very specific outfit. You can often know the social status of a woman in wealth based on who her hairdresser is. Hair is not over-processed, though it *is* colored to have a natural look. Hair tends to be chin length. An excellent hairdresser can give you exactly the same cut at least three times (that is the delineator). The cut falls naturally, no matter how you shake your head. Jewelry is minimal. "No diamonds before 5 p.m." is often used as a guideline. A good watch is a must. Nails are kept fairly short and manicured. Polish is clear.

The Shame of Not Belonging

Emotionally, appearance can be a source of pain, as well as pride and pleasure. Clothing is one of the quickest cues to determine class. It's a dead giveaway of where people do and don't fit in on so many levels. When people don't know the hidden rules—or know them and don't have the financial resources to follow through on them—they often feel embarrassed because their ignorance or deficiency has been exposed. An educational consultant on my staff shares the following perspective.

> When I got my doctorate, at first my mother wouldn't come to the graduation. I found out later that my mother-in-law made her come. At the time I thought she had refused because she was critical and didn't appreciate my education. In reality, she felt uncomfortable in an auditorium of strangers, as she only had a sixth-grade education. What made it worse was that she didn't feel she had anything appropriate to wear. She also had

hardly any teeth because of lack of access to dental care. How hard it would have been for her! But she did go, and she had a good time. I just wish I'd have been sensitive enough then to know that her reluctance wasn't about not caring about me but those other issues.

In addition, the hidden rules of one class often don't make sense to people in another class. Take the following case, for example, from the wife of a minister.

After my husband became a youth minister in Oklahoma, he moved on to a seminary in Dallas in 1979. Although we were raising three children, we only had $880 dollars a month to live on while we were there. And we were far away from our families, so we didn't have their daily support. We spent two and a half years in situational poverty. The church where we worshipped was in an affluent area and the congregation sponsored us.

In retrospect, if I had known to, I would have liked to focus more on studying and watching the other church members to see how they did things versus being paranoid about circumstances. I thought too much about how I dressed, my shoes, and so forth. I was proud about my family and kids. But when you go to church with rich people, you can't help but look around and compare yourself. It felt as though we were "passing," even though they took us in and were kind.

Some ladies in the church broke the hidden rules of wealth to make me feel comfortable. One brought me stacks of boys' clothes. She had older children, a couple of years ahead of mine. She didn't want to offend me or embarrass me, so she left the clothes in the trunk of her car. It was a secret passing of clothes. It broke a rule for her, because there are no hand-me-downs in wealth. I think she wanted to make me feel better. Oddly, the play clothes she gave us were actually what my own kids would have worn to church. My kids didn't like wearing ties. We had middle-income requirements.

In *Your* Life . . .

If you're from middle class and marry someone from poverty, clothes may be an issue. Your spouse won't understand the cost and amount of money spent on clothing suitable for a particular position. In this case you may prefer to do as my friend has. She said, "My husband and I have always had a good relationship. But the most difficult thing to adjust to was each other's attitudes. So we divided tasks according to which one of us does them best—and what's most important to each of us. I shopped for the kids' clothes and his clothes, as such things don't mean that much to him. The stuff I buy for him . . . well, he won't buy nice things for himself, as he feels they're too extravagant."

As another acquaintance said, "Growing up, I recall that my family knew which stores sold the best clothes. We'd go buy the patterns to sew things. My grandma would rarely wear anything with a tag. That meant too much had been paid for it. She was a quilter and preferred homemade everything. We also shopped a lot at tag sales and rummage sales."

If you're moving from poverty to middle class, remember it's important that clothing have quality and a decent fit. One of the most common mistakes in the move from poverty to middle class is to buy clothing that's bigger than it needs to be *or* to wear clothing that's too tight (in other words, poorly fitted apparel). Women are advised to have a few pieces of good jewelry and not to wear too much at one time.

It's fascinating how attitudes about clothing are often a blend of class-driven hidden rules, particularly among middle-class young people, who may experiment to find their identity but often don't have much disposable cash in their pockets. As a mother who made the transition out of poverty noted, "It has been interesting watching our children, and how our earlier situational poverty affected them. Their strong formative years—ages three to five and five to seven— were during the time when my husband and I went to school. They knew and understood 'lean,' and the necessity of rolling quarters to get groceries. Now that they're grown, they have eclectic tastes in clothes. They may shop at the local Gap and then mix it up with an item of clothing from Goodwill or the Salvation Army."

If you're moving from middle class to wealth, you should know that clothing should be chosen for its fit, artistic merit, and design. The fabric should be wool, silk, linen, or cotton. How much it will cost to take care of the clothing is not a factor in the decision making. An excellent fit is *essential*, as are the lines. The quality of the workmanship should be examined. Suggestion: Read John Molloy's books for men and women called *Dress for Success* (see Bibliography).

If you're moving into wealth, also plan to obtain the services of a personal assistant and a tailor. Both will be important. A highly skilled tailor will help you understand color and fit. A personal assistant will help you select clothing that is appropriate. Go to Neiman Marcus, Saks Fifth Avenue, or Nordstrom's and ask for a personal assistant. Get a professional makeover. (It's free.)

Please remember: To avoid conflict with your significant other over the issue of appropriate attire, try to clarify expectations. If you're the one moving into unfamiliar territory, feel free to ask questions ahead of time and solicit a trusted opinion. Good beginning questions can be: "What are you wearing?" or "Is there a dress code?" Observe and mimic role models who move comfortably within that same community. If you're the one bringing someone you care about from another class background into your own social circles, make the situation easier on him/her by providing information about the experience ahead. Offering friendly advice is generally OK, so long as it is welcomed and you stick to communicating in a loving, non-critical tone.

CHAPTER 7

Furnishing and Decorating Your Home

*O*n a domestic relationship, different beliefs about how a home should be furnished and maintained can be a source of tension, unless you understand the hidden rules of class. Hidden rules extend to the appearance of the home in the same way that they underlie personal appearance. Homes reflect the personal resources and mindsets of their inhabitants, as well as their personalities. Interestingly, the economic classes utilize the five physical senses differently; sound levels and lighting may vary greatly. Furthermore, as we saw in Chapter 3, many thought processes influence decision-making. Choices about interior design incorporate the role of the senses, as well as degree of attention to detail, financial wherewithal, emotional matters, and more.

A colleague of mine, who made the jump from poverty to middle class, describes this interplay well.

Our homes have always been pretty creative. It was important to me to have what I consider a pretty and a comfortable environment because of my circumstances growing up. My husband had no interest in it. That was actually kind of a problem because I couldn't motivate him to want it like I did. He took it for granted. It really was important to me. Even as a teacher, it was important to me when I taught kids from poor areas that the classroom be a Better Homes and Gardens*–type environment— homey, inviting, and special—because I felt they needed beauty*

around them. A lot of times, the places where they lived were
bleak. My original home was like that.

Consider the following three scenarios.

Your living area is small and dark. The windows are covered. A couple of lights are available, but most of the light in the room emanates from the television set. The TV is on virtually every waking hour (and sometimes during sleeping hours too!). The table is covered with papers; a small space has been cleared out to put a plate. The sink is piled high with dishes. There's a path around the chairs, and bags are in the corner full of clothes from a garage sale two weeks ago. Food from the grocery store is in some sacks on the kitchen floor where an overflowing trashcan also sits open.

Your living area has a great deal of light and the carpet is a light beige. The room has several lamps, and the furniture is color-coordinated. Reprints are used for pictures on the walls, and there are many knickknacks in various places, such as on the tables, bookshelves, and so on. You try to keep it neat, yet it still can get messy whenever you find yourself short on time to take care of it, along with your other daily obligations.

Your living area is spacious and light. Floor coverings are either stone or wood and covered with hand-loomed carpets of wool or silk. Furniture is designer-made, and the room makes a striking visual statement. Original art is displayed. Your domestic staff makes sure the space is immaculate and suitable for entertaining guests.

Explanation

Due to limited finances in poverty, efforts are made to ensure that utility bills are kept as low as possible. Therefore, lights are used only as needed, rooms are normally left dark to keep them cool, and furniture is functional rather than decorative. Furniture is viewed as part of a woman's domain and, if money is spent on furniture, it's minimal. Furniture is often purchased used, or it's obtained when someone moves. It isn't expected to fit a décor or match any kind of color scheme. As long as it doesn't have holes in it or isn't obviously broken, you consider it OK. If a sudden move is required, furniture is often left behind because of the difficulty in getting a truck or locating enough people to move the larger items. Your apartment or home tends to be rented and is rarely purchased. You're glad if the plumbing, heating, and air conditioning work.

In middle class the home is an extension of you and reflects the quality you can afford and the taste you have. Not only your home itself has value, so also does the acreage or the subdivision where you live. Furniture is an investment and is sometimes financed on payments. Furniture is evaluated both for its appearance and fit within the décor. Decisions about furniture are made as a couple— or at least with your spouse/partner in mind. Furniture is kept for many years—sometimes for the life of the relationship (for example, bedroom suites and dining room furniture). Wallpaper is frequently used. If the residence is new, the house plans are generally purchased and are not unique to that dwelling. If the house has been previously owned, renovations are usually done by the homeowners themselves and reflect their capabilities. The homeowners often do landscaping, but it tends to be minimal.

In wealth the address of your home is important. Furniture in your house is usually by a particular designer, and it customarily consists of predominantly one-of-a-kind pieces or antiques. "Provenance" is kept with the furniture, as are the records of purchases and sales. (Provenance is a piece of paper identifying the originator of an object, the previous owners, any changes to the original object, purchase prices, and current value.) Many fewer pieces of furniture are used in wealth, and a great deal of space is given to the display of original art. Space, light, and design are fundamental aspects in the décor. Furnishings are selected to play off them. Original materials (wood, stone, plaster, silk, and wool) are preferred for the floors and walls.

Decisions about the furnishings are usually a joint decision of a couple, and these are seldom made without in-depth conversation with designers. In addition, an architect designs a home and it is unique. A landscape architect is also used. In close consultation with the owners, the architect, landscape architect, and interior design firm all work together to create the home. If a previously owned dwelling is bought, a decision is made as to its architectural soundness. If the structure is architecturally sound, it will be renovated following strict standards of authenticity. If the house is not architecturally sound, it will be razed and a new one built. When a home is sold, the furniture is generally sold with it because furnishings were purchased for that particular space and design.

In *Your* Life . . .

If you're from poverty and moving into middle class, expect that money will be spent on a house and its furnishings—and that items will be updated over time. As my husband said to me after we had our home for about a year, "We'll never be finished, will we?" I replied, "You're correct."

In addition, a level of quality is expected. Furnishing two bedrooms, a living room, and a dining room will equal the cost of a car. If you're from poverty, that will seem excessive. In middle class, despite all the alterations and renovations, one would not spend more on decorating and furnishings than the cost of the home.

Another surprise about home ownership for those moving from poverty to middle class is the cost of insurance, maintenance, and upkeep. Frequently you find that you can't do everything yourself, and you need to hire help. This may rub you the wrong way. Frank and I live on an acre of land. It takes seven or eight hours to take care of the yard. Nonetheless, he didn't want to hire a yard service. He doesn't like having people other than family or friends in or around the house, whereas I view their presence as a tradeoff for freedom to pursue other activities.

I pointed this out: "Honey, you just don't have time." He has a construction company and is building properties. "Do you really have time to do this chore?"

He replied, adamantly, "I sure do."

"OK then," I conceded, "but I'm not living in a place that looks like this! So we either get yard service or you do it." The yard looked truly awful.

He muttered. Then we got a yard service.

If you're from middle class and marry into wealth, the cost of furnishing and decorating your home is often considerably greater than the purchase price of the home. The details and expertise of the finishing will be highly important. Expect to spend at least the purchase price of the home on furnishings, decorating, and landscaping (unless they're purchased as a complete package). The price of such a package can be two to three times the cost of the home.

Middle-class people typically calculate whether they can afford a home. But in wealth the purchase price is rarely an issue. The real costs are for furnishings, security, domestic support, maintenance, and insurance—the most important being security.

The Role of the Senses—Especially Noise and Lighting

Imagine you're watching TV, and it's late. You usually seem to fall asleep with the TV on. You like the background noise that it makes. During the day you keep both the radio and TV on at the same time, and you sometimes turn them up so you can't hear the bed squeaking as your brother and his wife make love in the next room. In fact, you really can't sleep without the TV on. You yell at your wife as she leaves the room to make the kids quit screaming.

You're watching TV, and it's late. You have the remote in the bed with you and, as soon as the evening news is over, you turn it off. You have a book by the bed that you're reading as well. The children are in the other part of the house asleep. The news is over. You turn off the TV. The house is quiet for the night. You've picked up the house, the dishwasher has run, the doors are locked, the garage door is closed, and the children have selected clothes to wear to school in the morning.

You're watching TV, and it's late. The flat screen is on the wall and you have programmed it to shut off automatically if the last show you have on is the evening news. The nanny has informed you that the children are asleep. You're also informed that the security system has been set for the evening. And you've set the intercom system to alert you if there's a problem in any area of the 25-room house.

In *Your* Life . . .

In poverty the noise level is higher than in middle class. Radios, TVs, and CD players tend to be louder, partly because they drown out other noises. In poverty the sense of hearing and the sense of smell are relied upon more than in middle class. It's fairly easy for someone to hide visually because poor neighborhoods tend to have less lighting than more affluent areas. One of the ways you survive potential danger is to pay attention to smells and sounds.

If you're from middle class and marry into poverty, expect that your spouse won't know when a light bulb has burned out. It simply won't be noticed. Furthermore, expect that he/she will speak louder in conversation at times than you would like.

In middle class visual discrimination becomes much more important, and visual clutter is *verboten*. Middle-class homes tend to be quiet when people are sleeping. They have more lighting elements than homes in poverty, and more contrasting color. If you're from poverty and marry into middle class, understand that your spouse will be quite concerned with the way things look. Light will be very important.

The aesthetic ambiance of the home—the use of space and light and color—is vital in affluence and, therefore, the visual senses are highly developed. In wealth individuals speak more softly and quietly to each other than in middle class. Part of the reason is that if you want privacy from the domestic staff, you must lower your voice. If you're marrying into wealth, speak more softly and quietly than has been customary.

CHAPTER 8

Getting Along with Your In-Laws

rank was the child that Mommy figured she could always talk to; he would understand. So when he went into the military, she and I got pretty close. I'd go over to her house in the evening after I taught school for the day, we'd make sandwiches, and then we'd sit on the front porch and talk. She was an astute observer and made predictions about people in the neighborhood. "See that guy over there? Well, let me tell you what he's going to do next." And: "That girl is going to be pregnant before the year's out." The people would do it.

There was also a lot that Mommy didn't tell me. She'd skirt around the edges of certain things, and I didn't really understand. For example, she'd call Frank sometimes in the middle of the night. He'd get out of bed and say, "I've got to go over to Mommy's."

"What's wrong?" I would ask.

"Oh, nothing you need to worry about." He'd go over and come back after a couple of hours. I knew something had happened, but there was a tacit agreement between him and his mother that I wasn't to be told. I was curious. I knew he wasn't getting up in the middle of the night because things were fine. But in poverty, when bad stuff happens, the family has a way of closing ranks for protection. The belief is: You wouldn't really understand anyway. You couldn't possibly understand.

Later on I found out what had actually occurred. I got parts of stories for many, many years that I finally was able to string together. This tendency to mask sad events and circle around them in stories is why the research on poverty is basically so weak. A research study is done for only a couple of years, and you can mask a lot of your business for that length of time. The reason I finally got inside knowledge was that I married Frank. As stuff slowly surfaced, I began asking questions and seeking answers.

When we marry, not only do we marry our spouse for better or for worse, we also marry our in-laws. The extended family can be a major asset in the form of a support system; it also can place a tremendous strain on a couple. Lots of marriages break up under the pressures of coping with family issues. This problem can be particularly hard if there is dysfunctional behavior going on, such as addictions and abuse.

Frank's mother loved me—*and* she liked me—and she helped me along the way. If Mommy had hated me, it would have been a lot more difficult, if not almost impossible for the marriage to survive, because we had opposition from my side of the family. They absolutely did not want me to marry Frank.

There would've been a fistfight at our wedding if my family had believed in fighting. My dad was a Mennonite minister, and Mennonites are pacifists. We rented a chapel, as my parents would not let me be married in their church because they disapproved of Frank and his family. The Mennonites sat on one side, and the hillbillies sat on the other. There was no conversation between the two. I was so glad when the reception was over. It was a tense event, to say the least.

Later on, my parents came to love Frank. He bought my mother a new stove, so now he can safely go to heaven before me, of course; he's at the front of the line. And we bought them a car, which my dad thinks is wonderful. They're in their 80s, and we want them to be happy. They've been excellent grandparents to our son, Tom.

Time changes everything.

Three Typical Scenarios

Imagine that your mother-in-law calls your husband every morning and talks to him for 20 minutes. She tells him everything that happened in the family and the neighborhood yesterday. Today she tells him to stop by after work and have a cup of coffee with her. She is very upset. His brother (her other son) hasn't been by to see her for three days. They had a big fight, and she tells your husband, "He can't come to my funeral!" She says, "Ask your wife why she didn't come see me yesterday." Later in the day she calls you and tells you to pick her up at 6 o'clock on Saturday morning and take her to a garage sale. She doesn't drive. You know that if you don't take her she'll make your life miserable all week.

Your mother-in-law called your husband last week and invited him to Sunday dinner two weeks from now. His sister and her husband are visiting from out of state with their new infant, and she's planning a family dinner. You ask if there's anything you should bring, and she suggests you bring the dessert. You aren't crazy about your new brother-in-law, but you figure that a couple of hours on Sunday won't kill you.

Your mother-in-law calls your husband to remind him of the table he's hosting at the political luncheon she's sponsoring for the incumbent mayor. Plates are $100 per attendee, and he's hosting a table for eight. In addition, she inquires about the children and your wife—and would it be possible to go sailing with them this weekend? You tell her you'll check the calendar and have your secretary get back with her.

Explanation

In all economic classes, family dynamics vary from family to family. Identity, intimacy, and independence are interwoven. These factors spring from early family understandings and often are evidenced by the internal and external boundaries that are displayed. The more dysfunctional the family, the greater the boundary issues.

In one person's words, "I was an abused child—physically and psychologically abused—because my mother was so desperately unhappy. She took it out on me. I was a possession. That doesn't quit when you become an adult. Sometimes to hurt *me* (particularly because my mother knew I thought it was important for my children to have a relationship with her), she wouldn't buy the kids presents at Christmas. So I'd go out and buy them presents in her name."

One definition of dysfunction is the extent to which virtually all of one's own needs are sublimated to meet the needs of another (or others). If there are addictions, extreme poverty, biochemical issues, societal oppression, extreme medical needs, abuse, extreme religious involvement, and so on, then the internal and external boundaries are breached and stretched, or become rigid or nonexistent. In these cases, seeking the professional help of a psychotherapist or spiritual counselor is highly recommended.

In poverty, as a basic guideline, the structure of the family tends to be more matriarchal, although men are given more freedom. In middle class the family structure tends to be more patriarchal with both sexes held equally responsible. In wealth there is a greater level of independence, in part dependent on who has the money. Women in wealth are given a great deal of deference and latitude.

In generational poverty, within the family structure and among the in-laws, there is often a lot of open infighting. There will be verbal and physical fights. Family members will take sides against other family members. There will be periods of time when one family member doesn't speak to another family member. The mother is considered to be "keeper of the soul" and has a great deal of clout.

In middle class, within the family structure and among the in-laws, there is less open fighting and more avoidance. If there is someone you don't like, you may discreetly discuss that individual with another family member, but you would not openly take such a person on at a family gathering. You may leave the social event early or, as noted, talk to someone else. Sometimes the latter action is called "triangling." It isn't a healthy dynamic. This is when two people join together against a third person. And the two people on a side usually keep changing. It's a survival strategy. There is power in numbers.

In wealth, if there is enmity between family members or in-laws, it typically shows up in legal battles, proxy fights, and rivalries through charities. However, you remain polite and keep up appearances at social and family gatherings.

In *Your* Life . . .

If you come from middle class and marry or otherwise move into poverty, don't take sides. Be too busy with your own life to participate in the battles. There will be constant battles and, most of the time, they are unresolved (and irresolvable). Keep the disagreements in your own relationship out of the family gossip mill. It will only complicate things when your spouse's siblings feel they need to take sides. When you do resolve your difficulties, they'll still have their feelings and preconceived notions to get over.

If you're female, you'll need to come to come to a private peace about the role of your husband's mother in his life and, therefore, in your life. Furthermore, it isn't unusual in poverty to have favorite children. Kids frequently are compared. For example: "This is my good son." Or . . . "He's the bad seed (or black sheep)." Or . . . "She never was nice and pretty like her sister." Favoritism regarding children creates jealousy among the siblings, as well as the in-laws. Understand that this may happen. Don't allow it to affect your neutrality. Easier said than done, of course.

"My in-laws don't act proud of my husband, even though he has been successful," a woman I met at a seminar told me. "When I think about it, it hurts. His sisters have alcohol and drug problems. One sister has illegitimate children with three different men . . . But they're not proud of my husband. One time his mom hit the nail on the head. She said, 'We ignore you because you're OK.' "

You may be asked to have family members come live with you. You will need to reach an understanding with your partner/spouse about that. You will probably be asked to get family members and/or in-laws out of jail. Again, you'll need to come to an agreement with your partner/spouse.

I'll never forget. We had been married about a year when we got a call in the middle of the night that Frank's brother had been arrested for drinking and busting heads, and he needed $500 to bail him out of jail. Frank woke me up and said, "We're going to need the checkbook. Would you go get it?"

Well, I was up in a flash. "Five hundred dollars! That's a lot of money." I was making just $7,500 a year as a teacher. I said, "We need to talk about this."

He said, "Yes we do. Ruby, if he's not at work on Monday, he's fired. I don't agree with what he's done ... but I can't in good conscience let his wife and son go homeless. We can give him the money, or the boy can come live with us."

Wow, this IS serious, I thought. I immediately started looking for the checkbook.

"Ruby, he's got a child. We can't let that boy starve. If my brother loses his job—because he's got a child—it's going to change *our* whole financial picture."

As he was leaving, I asked Frank, "Do you think $500 is enough?" I was willing to donate more to the cause.

If you grew up in poverty and move into middle class, understand that most middle-class families don't operate in crisis mode. They aren't unfeeling. There just isn't the emotional roller-coaster ride to which you may be accustomed. Feelings are sublimated to issues. An open physical fight would rarely happen, and verbal battles usually wouldn't be prolonged. The "he-said-she-said-they-said" conflicts tend to be quickly discovered and dismissed for lack of evidence!

If you come from middle class and marry into wealth, understand that there's a "class mask" and that emotional responses are muted among the wealthy. So while there is *not* ice water in their veins, most rich folks *are* very controlled with their emotional expressions. Precise language is valued, so descriptions of incidents, people, and so on are specific and prudent. Carefully chosen words convey likes and dislikes.

CHAPTER 9

Hidden Rules of Raising Children

arents of every class love their children. For almost all parents, children are the deepest source of joy and/or sorrow in their lives. But the significance of having children and the greater meaning of children may vary by class. Consider the typical scenarios below.

You and your partner really want children. You want a son, and all your buddies laugh and say you must be "shooting blanks." Before you were in a relationship you didn't really care that you didn't father a child. But now you want one. You wouldn't adopt. You want it to be your own flesh-and-blood son. You wonder if the problem is your partner. But you wouldn't consider going to a doctor to find out. You don't want him messing with anyone's privates—yours or your partner's.

Or ... your partner is pregnant again. It's your fourth child. What the hell happened? You thought she was on the pill, but she forgot to take it. You didn't use protection. After all, it's her job to take care of it if she doesn't want to "blow up like a balloon" again. You had a big fight when you found out. You blamed her, she blamed you. Yet another mouth to feed; sometimes it's just too much. You don't have insurance either. You had a fight with the boss and quit the last job where you did have insurance. The job you now have is part-time and doesn't come with insurance.

You and your partner really want children. You don't care about the sex of the child as long as it's healthy. You and your partner have gone to several infertility specialists to determine the problem. Both you and your partner have had several tests done. You're willing to adopt *if* you can get a healthy child. It's very expensive, but you're willing to do it. You're also willing to adopt a child from another country.

Or . . . your partner is pregnant again. Neither of you is happy about it. It will be your fourth child and, while you have insurance, you clearly understand the financial costs. You're not sure how you're going to pay for college. You realize it will now be at least another five years before you can retire. You know you'll love and care for the child. It's just that the financial implications are almost overwhelming.

You and your partner want children but, after a year of trying, there's no pregnancy. The two of you have been to several clinics and learn that, in this case, she's infertile. To ensure the health of an adopted child, you make a major donation to a premier adoption agency. You're very specific about the health of the mother and prenatal care. You also carefully analyze the child's genetic background before giving your approval. The adoption will be extremely expensive, but you can afford it. You and your partner also look into using your sperm and having the fetus carried by a surrogate mother. Then, as a couple, at least half of your genetic lineage would be perpetuated.

Or . . . your partner is unexpectedly pregnant. This is your fourth child. You discuss your options. She is particularly concerned about the effects on her body as she approaches her 40th birthday. There will not be a financial issue with the child.

Explanation

In poverty, children are seen as proof of being a "real man" or a "real woman." In fact, a significant rite of passage in poverty is to father a child or give birth to a child. For a male from poverty, a son is often seen as proof of virility. A child is clearly seen as a possession, and it's acceptable to hit your child as a part of discipline.

Children are viewed as both gift and responsibility in middle class. So time and money are spent developing your children. You buy them tennis lessons and swimming lessons, pay for college, and so forth. Rites of passage in middle class for growing children are getting a job, driver's license, high school diploma, or college degree.

In wealth, children are viewed as the continuation of the lineage. A rite of passage in wealth is when adult children begin to accrue interest from their trust funds (usually around age 21) and then, more importantly, when they gain control of the principal of their trust funds (often around 35).

Differences between and among the classes are not as pronounced at the elementary school level because parents are more clearly controlling the agenda at that stage in life. However, wealthy adolescents and teens live in a world that their peers in poverty—and even the middle class—can scarcely imagine. From sailing the small islands of the South Pacific, to working on a world-renowned archeological dig, to taking private pitching lessons from baseball Hall of Fame strike-out leader Nolan Ryan, to being a page for a U.S. senator, rich kids enjoy almost limitless material resources and travel opportunities.

It also must be noted that in all classes there are some parents who don't parent well—parents who don't provide the structures and attention needed for the multi-faceted growth of children. This happens when parents exempt the child from responsibility, demand too much of the child, or don't offer the support and nurture necessary for healthy development.

An Old-Money Story

Charles, age 24, is third-generation money. Both his parents came from money. His paternal grandfather made the original family fortune. A trust fund was established at Charles' birth, and he also was named in earlier trusts as "future progeny." At age 21 he began receiving a monthly check from the interest on his trust funds, but he won't control the principal until he's 35. Twice a year, Charles meets with his trust adviser (in this case, his father) and a lawyer to update the fund's holdings.

A great deal of Charles' time is currently spent in social activities, but he uses his social and financial connections in part to further his career as a playwright. Charles is a bit unusual for his social group in that he wants to be an acclaimed writer. He knows he can be published—he has enough connections to ensure that—but he wants to be celebrated. He attended private boarding school and graduated from Yale University, as did his father. By 30 it's expected that he'll participate in one of the family businesses.

Charles' hobbies are sailing, golf, ballooning, flying, skiing, and the theater. He spends part of the year in Palm Springs, California; part of the year in Aspen and Vail, Colorado; part of the year in Europe; and part of the year in New York City. In addition, he travels either first class or, more often, in the corporate or family jet. Domestic help takes care of everything: his clothing, cleaning, meals, and so on. A tailor makes his clothes, often selecting both fabric and style, as he knows Charles' personal tastes. At one family estate, an individual is hired full-time just to keep the pool area clean, fold the towels, and so forth. Another employee has a full-time job polishing the brass.

Charles' allowance is $10,000 a month. He doesn't have bills because he always lives in one of the family homes or apartments around the world—and doesn't pay for utilities or other expenses. Additionally, he has been "gifted" a couple of residences. The family pays for his private club memberships, and one of his cars was a gift at college graduation. Charles has no debt. The family accounting and law firms manage his trust funds.

Right now he's involved in a lawsuit against his own family. His father divorced his mother when he was ten years old and married a much younger woman. Now his father has two children by his new wife. When his parents got divorced, there was an ugly battle. Several years ago Charles had lunch with his father, who made an offhand comment that bothered him. So Charles hired another attorney to investigate the status of his trust funds. The lawyer found out that his father had established an elaborate paper game. Charles' trusts, intended to have assets of $1 billion, have assets of only $180 million.

In short, the family has about 100 trust funds—several of which are offshore and overseas—that were created before the Internal Revenue Service understood them. Consequently these trusts were "grandfathered" into the law, meaning they don't have to conform to current statutes. Charles' father set up more trusts, then set up banks to house the money from the trusts. After that he established new businesses whose primary funding came from the banks that took money from the trusts. Charles' original trusts provided a great deal of start-up capital to businesses that didn't make money, so they weren't being reimbursed.

Furthermore, Charles found out that his father had "gifted" $200 million to his current wife's mother. The $200 million was a loan that was never paid back. Thus, it became a gift. It was written off as bad debt.

When he was 21 Charles started the lawsuit. It has been going on for three years. He is seeking to have the original money reinstated to his trust funds and to assume control over it. Charles knows this will be a huge battle. His father previously waged a decades-long battle against the IRS over what the IRS said were insufficient tax payments.

A consequence of the lawsuit is that a few of Charles' club memberships have been pulled, so he must now pay the club fees himself. In the divorce his mother was wise and got several club memberships for life, which she extends to her son. However, several family members no longer speak to him. Charles expects to be mostly alone by the time the fight is finished. But he's determined to win, even though he knows the battle will get ugly. The part Charles likes the least is that the lawsuit has been discussed and examined in publications like the *New York Times, Business Week,* and *Forbes.*

Charles mostly spends his time with old-money friends like himself—or friends from the theater world. He doesn't need to worry that they'll make fun of him for his taste in clothes or art ... or that they'll want to use him for money. Charles has learned to be very careful and guard his privacy. Since the legal fight started, he has secured (through a court order) a bodyguard to be paid for directly from his trust. Further, he doesn't take calls. All calls are forwarded to the lawyer handling the lawsuit against his father. The lawyer's secretary screens the calls for Charles, passing on to him only those messages that she's sure he'll want to receive.

In *Your* Life . . .

If you're from middle class and marry someone from poverty, expect issues around how your children are disciplined. Your spouse likely will have a strong inclination to use physical means to punish children. The question I ask when parents say they must hit their children is this: "What will you do when they're too big to hit?" I go on to say, "Wouldn't it be better to give them the skills now so they can make good decisions when they're too big to hit? Teach your children choices, consequences, and parameters."

If you're from poverty and moving into middle class, understand that the development of the children through education, lessons, team sports, and so on will be very important. Time and money will be devoted to that effort. You may not believe it, but when your wife learns that your ten-year-old forgot to do his school assignment that's due the next day, she'll stay up half the night and work with that child till it's done. As you may recall, I helped Tom build a replica of the Great Wall of China with poster board.

If you're moving from middle class into wealth, understand that deference will be given to your children, yet a higher level of responsibility will be demanded of those children at the same time. Children in wealth are groomed to carry on family traditions and demonstrate accomplishments that reflect well on parents and relatives (look, for example, at the Kennedy and Bush families). Grown children are expected to establish and maintain connections that preserve family assets.

Your Child's Education

It's time for your child to go to public school kindergarten. You walked to the barbershop, and you see a sign that says kindergarten "roundup" is on Monday. You're supposed to register your child.

But the car isn't running, and you don't have a ride. So you wait until the end of the summer and put your child on the bus. He brings a bunch of papers home for you to sign. You hear from the neighbors that the teacher is new. As long as your child likes the teacher, it's fine. You know that going to school doesn't make much difference in a person's life. It sure didn't for you. And you don't know anyone it *did* make a difference for.

It's time for your child to go to public school kindergarten. You've had her in a preschool for two years now, and she knows her letters and numbers—and she can read some words. You register her for kindergarten and take her with you so she'll feel comfortable at school. You're very concerned about who the teacher is going to be and check around at the soccer game for recommendations about teachers. You go to the principal and request the recommended teacher. In addition, you seek out the teacher privately and explain the educational background of your daughter, along with a few special issues that pertain to her. You know how important the teacher is to the success of your child.

It's time for your child to go to private kindergarten. You've had your son's name on the list of this private school since his birth. You understand how essential the right private school is to the rest of his life, particularly the social connections that will be made. You have participated in all the fund-raisers and have donated countless hours to volunteer activities for this private school. You understand that there are a finite number of students the school can take. Your son gets in. You breathe a sigh of relief. Next year he will go to a private boarding school.

Explanation

In generational poverty, education is often feared because when children become educated, they leave. Then you have lost your possessions. In situational poverty, getting educated is encouraged because it's one of the best ways out of poverty.

In middle class, education is seen as the key to moving up the ladder. Not only is the degree important, the school and your child's teachers are considered vital as well. Furthermore, the higher-education setting is important, particularly the specific college or university and its reputation in that discipline. The biggest concern among middle-class families is paying for college. Loans often are taken out for the education of the children. Sometimes a savings account is set up soon after a child's birth to pay for higher education.

In wealth the particular private boarding school is key. It's the early identification of the connections that children will need in their life. This will determine university admittance, sorority and fraternity invitations, and so forth. Later in life all kinds of important connections will result from the initial boarding school experience.

In *Your* Life . . .

If you're from middle class and marry someone from poverty, don't expect your spouse to understand the significance of the teacher or the school. This will become your responsibility, and you periodically will need to address this issue yourself.

If you're from poverty and marry into middle class, your spouse/partner almost certainly will be adamant about the importance of educational opportunities. When you buy a house, the school and educational system will be front and center. Your spouse will spend time finding out who the teacher and principal are. Middle-class parents frequently talk about such things at social, religious, and sports gatherings.

If you're from middle class and marry into wealth, expect that your child will go to a private boarding school. A friend of mine grew up middle class and married into wealth. Soon after their son was born, her husband said to her, "We need to enroll him now in boarding school so that he'll go there when he's six years old." She started crying and said, "I can't send him away when he's only six. I can't stand it. I'll get a divorce before I let that happen." They finally compromised: Their child would go to boarding school at age eight, the start of third grade.

CHAPTER 10
Work and Your Desire to Achieve

*W*ork has many dimensions, and these have a strong impact on our relationships. First of all, it's one of the ways that we can generate income and are able to support our families and ourselves. Unless we're independently wealthy, we need to work so we can take care of the basic human needs for food, shelter, and clothing, as well as pay the bills that we incur. Work is also one of the ways we can make a positive contribution to the world, and it gives us feelings of satisfaction, confidence, and accomplishment. This is true for both paid employment and volunteer work. Additionally, the work we do is a major element in our personal identity. It can afford us status and a sense of membership in a community.

On the negative side, work puts assorted pressures on us. It detracts from the time we can spend with our significant others and children. This can create distance in a marriage or romantic relationship. It requires that we already possess or are willing to learn certain skills and abilities. And, in many cases, it demands that we subordinate ourselves to other people—and/or supervise them and assume responsibility. In order to climb the economic ladder, we need to embrace at least some hidden rules of the class above ours. Accepting and learning to live with these realities can make everything flow more smoothly.

How do people from the different classes handle workplace conflicts? Here's an extreme example (true story) that illustrates the clash of values and hidden rules between poverty and middle class.

A field-service hand of an oil company comes into the main office and starts flirting with one of the secretaries. He tells her about the "f---ing" work, how "f---ing" hard it is, and what a "s---head" the boss is. After a few moments, the secretary says to him, "I don't appreciate your language; I find it offensive." The man looks at her in disbelief, then turns to another secretary and asks, "What the f--- did I *say*?"

Here's a more typical example from poverty.

Your boss has been harassing you again. You got this job because of your brother, but you hate his boss. He likes the boss, but the boss leaves *him* alone. You would like to quit, but you know your brother would quit too, and you don't want that to happen because he likes his job. You call a friend and tell him, "I think I have a job I can't quit." But a couple of weeks later, you get mad at the boss and quit on the spot. Your brother quits too.

Now consider this middle-class equivalent. Your boss has been harassing you again. He's a control freak and micromanages everything. He requires you to give him a detailed daily list of what you've accomplished. You have a master's degree in business administration, yet he watches you like a hawk. You decide you must find a different boss or go to another company. You contact friends within the professional organizations that you belong to, and you look at employment opportunities in the paper and online. You have a mentor whom you talk to about the situation, and he gives you coping mechanisms you can use until you can find another position.

In wealth a personal confrontation might resemble the following scenario. You're on the board of directors, and you don't like the chief executive officer of the corporation. You question his integrity and leadership. You're becoming increasingly convinced that he isn't paying appropriate dividends and that shareholder value is diminishing. Rumor also has it that the CEO has an "assistant," a female corporate vice president who travels everywhere with him. Moreover, the CEO has issued a corporate report that is less than transparent. In your role on the board, you've been seeking better information. The CEO has managed to thwart your every move—

and lately won't even return your phone calls and e-mail messages —so you decide to mount a proxy fight at the next meeting of the board of directors.

Explanation

In poverty the philosophy about work usually is that "you were looking for a job when you found this one." Getting to work on time is often a problem. The car is a recurring headache. It frequently won't start. You clock in, you clock out. You get paid by the hour, and you get paid for overtime. The only reason you work is to see your friends there and make some money. Work is for survival. If other sources of income are possible (unemployment benefits, workers' compensation, disability, and so on), those will be used. It isn't unusual to go for periods of time without work or to be looking for work. Additionally, in poverty, if you don't like the boss, you quit. It doesn't matter whether you have another job lined up; you simply quit.

An educational colleague describes how she and her husband had tried to mentor two of his nephews, both of whom grew up in poverty.

> We gave the boys as much exposure to the middle class and our lifestyle as we could. They came for holidays. But they never lived with us. They're in their 30s now. The younger one got a high school degree and works as an assistant manager in a fast food chain, but he hasn't set his sights higher.
>
> The older nephew got involved in a drug scam and was incarcerated for two years. When he got out of prison, we gave him a job at the catering business we owned. We felt that providing him a job and a place to stay would give him a chance to save money and time to get on his feet. But in his head, the young man could never get there. He couldn't get past the "hustler" inside him. We asked him to move out.
>
> Then the older nephew got in more trouble. He tried to rob an off-duty police officer. He stole a car and drove it back to our

*house. There were actually SWAT teams in the yard. He was in
so much trouble then that we couldn't help get him out of it. My
husband is angry that the boy's father didn't take a more active
role in his upbringing. This child loved his dad dearly. But in the
poverty mindset, kids get to a certain age, and then they're on
their own. The father basically abandoned both boys when he
split up with their mother.*

In middle class the philosophy about work is that it's a career.
You don't expect to stay with the same company for 45 years, but
you do expect to be doing the kind of work you like. You look for
opportunities for varied career experiences that will enhance your
résumé—and that are personally rewarding and satisfying for you.
You work for the money you earn, but the personal satisfaction and
learning are equally important. Work tends to be a positive source
of identity.

In wealth the philosophy about work is that it should have
meaning. You don't need the money *per se,* but you need the meaning, the fulfillment, and the connections that work offers. Your
work is about making a difference for a corporation and/or a cause.
While the money is important, you would work for less money. It's
a way of contributing to your community in particular and to society
in general.

Further, you understand the role of shareholder value and dividends. While you may have a great deal of net worth, you may not
always have income. Income is from the investments and is contingent on dividends and interest payments. Part of the "work" that
is done in wealth is ensuring corporate stability and responsibility.
Additionally, the "work" of wealth is to enhance national and international stability and responsibility. What is clearly understood is
that if the social or political well-being of a community, a country,
or even the world is upset, financial well-being can be affected or
even destroyed. Witness the collapse of the stock market in 1929 and
the ensuing Great Depression.

In *Your* Life . . .

If you're from middle class and marry into poverty, expect that your spouse/significant other will quit a job if he/she doesn't like the boss. The material security of the household will matter very little. Expect also that your spouse will turn down promotions if he/she doesn't like the boss or company. Finally, expect that he/she will find additional training or education highly "suspicious" and steer clear of it.

If you're from poverty and marry into middle class, expect that extra time will be given to the pursuit of the career. Classes will be taken, and long hours will be spent at work. Business trips will be required that may involve working with the opposite sex. It doesn't mean your spouse/significant other is cheating. It simply means he/she is probably working.

If you're from middle class and marry into wealth, understand how important your role is to your spouse's prospects for being promoted. As one business owner told me, "We don't promote to the executive level until we have met the spouse. The spouse is an indicator of the individual's judgment." Hence, the simple question, "He married *her*?" could doom a man's promotion potential. Or, conversely, "She married *him*?" could have the same effect.

Moreover, it's important to understand that the purpose of work at the executive level is not the same as at the mid-management level. If you look at the following chart, mid-management is about keeping track of projects, tasks, and so on. But the executive level is about keeping track of systems and connections.

Table 3 on pages 104 to 107 categorizes differences arising in four tiers of the workplace.

Time: Achievement vs. Relationships

Formal education is the piece of the economic puzzle that enables people to make the transition from poverty to middle class. Education is basic preparation for entering the workforce in that it expands a person's mental resources—through reading, writing, and

Table 3. Differences in the Workplace

ISSUE	UNSKILLED LABOR	BEGINNING SUPERVISION
KNOWLEDGE LEVEL	What I can do.	What I can get others to do.
RESPONSIBILITIES	Completion of tasks.	Completion of group tasks. Recommendations about hiring and firing.
CONNECTIONS	Connections/camaraderie within group.	With your immediate boss and group you are supervising.
PROTOCOL/CULTURE	Accepted norms of immediate working group.	Mix of what boss wants and norms of group.
FINANCIAL	Only as it relates to specific tasks.	Only as it relates to group task.
PLANNING	Daily, if any.	Planning for group tasks and task delegation.
TIME COMMITMENT	For hours paid.	Some overtime.
SCHOOLING	High school diploma or less.	High school or some college.*
RELOCATION	Not required.	Not required.

* Increasingly, two years of college is becoming a requirement for many occupations.

MID-MANAGEMENT	EXECUTIVE LEVEL
What I know.	Who I know.
Completion of projects and implementation of processes. Authority to hire and fire.	Identification of systems, products, services, and processes within business unit and among other related business units.
Internal connections up, down, and across organization crucial to success.	External connections vital to success of business unit.
Corporate hierarchy observed and followed.	National and often international social and business protocols observed and followed.
Departmental budget.	Profit and loss of business unit. Global strategic sales/revenues.
Weekly to annual. Project management.	Strategic. Quarterly to multi-year.
50-60 hours a week.	Position involves spouse, social activities, and extensive travel 60-80 hours a week.
Often a couple of years of college or college degree.	Often MBA.
May be required.	Required.

Table 3. Differences in the Workplace (continued)

ISSUE	UNSKILLED LABOR	BEGINNING SUPERVISION
TECHNICAL EXPERTISE	Not required but desirable.	Recommended.
COMMUNICATION	Mostly spoken, some written.	Responds in writing to written reports.
SPOUSE OR SIGNIFICANT OTHER	Does not matter.	Does not matter.
APPEARANCE	Needs to be somewhat clean.	Clean and presentable.

MID-MANAGEMENT	EXECUTIVE LEVEL
Use of specific software applications required.	Understanding and use of technical systems as they relate to strategic and financial success of business unit.
Produces written reports. Makes reports/presentations to peers, customers, subordinates, and executive level.	Analyzes corporate documents for effect/purpose. Makes reports/presentations to stakeholders.
Helpful but not crucial to career success.	Often determines whether promotion is given or not. Seen to reflect on person's judgment. Is reflection of personal choice.
Wears good-quality clothing that follows company norms and expectations. Clothing is pressed, neat, and clean.	Look is understated. Quality of haircut or hairstyle extremely important. Jewelry is limited to solid gold or platinum. Fit and quality of clothing and workmanship very important.

computing. If you are poorly educated, your skills will not be suitable for jobs that require mental acuity more than physical strength and dexterity. Believing in the value of learning is one of the main factors that distinguish the poverty mindset from the middle-class mindset. However, learning takes time. You must devote time to it that's unrelated to daily life. If you're operating in survival mode, you likely will feel that you cannot afford that time. Thus, school is not a priority in poverty, and academic achievement is not valued.

Success in school depends on being able to plan ahead to get projects and tasks done according to a specific time frame. As a student moves from being a novice to an accomplished learner, abstract concepts are naturally acquired. Being comfortable with abstractions is fundamental to the affluent world of finance and corporations, as all transactions takes place on paper or electronically on computer—stocks, bonds, treasury bills, financial spread sheets, and statistical reports, contracts and deeds, among other documents. (We'll take a closer look at the importance of abstract thinking in the next chapter.)

In wealth, achievement is measured by academic excellence; undergraduate, graduate, and postgraduate degrees from the finest colleges and universities; employment with the most prestigious firms; and membership in the most exclusive clubs. It's measured by your affiliations and charitable endeavors, as well as by sustaining traditions.

When making a transition from poverty to middle class or from middle class to wealth, much depends on your support systems, your relationships/role models, and your emotional resources. Without these resources, many people give up.

A teacher I met shares this story.

Back in the mid-'80s, because of company layoffs, my husband told me, "You go back to school and, as soon as I can, I will too. It will work with your mom living with us and helping with the kids." He helped me get through school, and I got a teaching certificate. Then, the semester before I graduated, he went back to school. He worked full time while he went, and I took over his responsibilities. Our children were seven and five. He worked 40 hours, and his employers let him off. In fact, they helped pay for the degree. We were both in school in our 30s. It was tough. School was about all we could do for two years. Thankfully, Mom was there and committed to helping us get through.

We were lucky to survive my husband's schooling. But we decided, "We'll stick it out." It helped that his employers were supportive of it and paying for it. His company promoted him afterward. He worked there for a while, then got a new job at a different company that was even better. He moved into management. Still, he once said to me, "I could've been a plant manager, but I started my education too late."

Typical Educational Scenarios

You have always wanted to be a teacher. You graduated from high school 20 years ago. You enroll in junior college and find out you have to take a year of remedial courses before you can begin a bachelor's degree. Your spouse is upset that you're back in school and taking time away from him. He gets put in jail, and you bail him out. He leaves you for a couple of months to live with another woman, and then he yells and cusses at you. He tells you that you don't love him, that you're an awful mother, and no kind of woman. Although you really want to be a teacher, you're thinking about quitting college.

You're going back to graduate school for a master's degree in business administration. Before you enroll in the program, you and your spouse discuss the time issues that will arise, particularly if/when you have a young child. Your spouse agrees to pick up more of the household tasks. Both of you understand that this degree will make a big difference in your future income. Because your place of employment will pay for the tuition, you don't need to worry about that. You apply to three programs and get accepted at two. You select a school and begin your graduate studies.

You've always known what institution you will attend for your undergraduate program. Your family has been a benefactor of this institution for some time. Furthermore, you're interested in a very particular field of study and have arranged for several summers to work with an expert in the field. Your main difficulty will be the necessity of attending a large number of social activities while pursuing this particular course of study.

Explanation

In poverty, it's important for things to remain the same to maintain a comfortable relationship. When one spouse or a child finds satisfaction outside the relationship through achievement, levels of uncertainty and anxiety often develop that create friction between the parties. The fear of losing your connection with the other person is so great that sometimes a spouse will give up the achievement to keep the relationship. The big fear is that you will "get above your raisings." When people get educated, they leave. So the fear of loss is real and often overwhelming.

Here's an illustration from a woman who grew up in poverty.

> *My mother discouraged me from getting an education. All the way through, she'd ask, "Why are you trying to get above your raisings? Why not stay home and raise your kids?" She was very critical. As a result, when I had to stand up for myself at work, I'd get sick to my stomach. No one knew, as I didn't share it, but that's the way it was. I hated it, because my stomach would ache. I know I can confront an issue, but it's always difficult for me. I do it because it's necessary and important. But I suffer. It's a conditioned response. I think a lot of that comes from having a mother who worked in a sweatshop and who criticized me for trying to better myself.*
>
> *I think the reason she criticized me was that, to her, it was important to be humble and to know your place. Part of that came from working in a factory. She put zippers in blue jeans on*

an assembly line. You can't keep a job in a plant if you're not submissive or if you raise problems for the floor managers. So it's hard for me too.

However, knowing that about myself, when my daughter would disagree with her dad and he started to rebuke her, I would take him in the bedroom and say, "She's bright, and she'll probably grow up to be an executive. So, as long as she's not disrespectful, you need to let her practice that skill of standing up to a man." I insisted, and he saw the reason in it. I didn't want her to have to go through the same physical pain as I have.

Many people in poverty choose not to go to school, or they quit school, for a very big reason. It's huge. To move from poverty to middle class or from middle class to wealth, there's a period of time in which you must trade many, if not all, of your relationships for achievement. You simply don't have time for both. Many people simultaneously work and go back to graduate school at night. Relationships are hard to maintain under those conditions, which can strain a marriage. Forget about dating.

In middle class, achievement is encouraged, as it enhances the opportunity for financial and social advancement. The expansion of opportunities allows new experiences that assist you as you move to the next position or level of achievement. What is clearly understood is that you'll spend less time on relationships to pursue achievement, but once your degree is obtained you'll go back to giving time to the relationships. While that doesn't always happen, middle-class people don't fear permanent loss to the same degree that those in poverty do.

In wealth it's expected that periods of time will be spent developing expertise, particularly in the arts. Development of that expertise won't necessarily cause you to be separated from relationships. Relationships often are maintained because the need to devote time to working for money isn't an issue. As we saw in the last chapter, children are usually in private boarding school, so their care doesn't place daily demands on your time. Certain social obligations must be addressed, unless you have established yourself apart from the social obligations.

In *Your* Life . . .

If you're from middle class and marry into poverty and you choose to go back to school, you'll need to explain in detail to your spouse exactly what you're doing and why. Ask your spouse/partner these questions: "How tough are you? Are you strong enough to have me gone most evenings so that eventually I can make more money?" Explain that a significant part of your motivation is that you're doing it for the children so they can be taken care of well.

A spouse can be an ally in the process of change, or a spouse can take an adversarial position. If conflict arises between you and your significant other that pertains to a desire for achievement and self-betterment, examine the emotional issues that such change triggers in both of you, along with the belief systems that are being brought to the fore.

If you want to encourage your significant other from a poverty background to focus on education, help him/her rethink and re-frame limiting beliefs, as follows: Education is a way to be admired. If you listen to the stories about heroes that are told in generational poverty, they tend to be either tricksters or anti-heroes like Robin Hood, who go up against society and win. To be either kind of hero, you have to be smarter. Anything that makes you smarter will make you admired. Being "successful," on the other hand, is a term that's often equated with being middle class. And it's not seen as desirable. Men in poverty have a polite term and a vulgar term for middle-class men. The polite term is "housebroken." The vulgar term is "p----whipped." You can figure out the rest.

If you're from poverty and marry into middle class, expect that you'll lose friends because you'll need to spend time in college and/or taking classes. (The 1997 movie *Good Will Hunting,* starring Matt Damon and Ben Affleck, dealt with these kinds of issues, particularly from a "guy" perspective.) As a friend of mine told me, "I can go back into their world, but they can't come into mine."

If you're from middle class and marry into wealth, develop an area of expertise that is respected, even revered, among the affluent. When you have the ability to purchase anything your heart desires, what distinguishes your lifestyle is the quality and beauty of your situation. To determine artistry and merit, you must have expertise. It can be either in a subject matter or in an area of responsibility. You can demonstrate expertise by preparing ahead of time by gathering stacks of books and magazines on a particular subject that's of interest to a person you're going to meet. Let him/her know you consulted experts and would like to discuss the information with him/her.

CHAPTER 11

Three Mindsets About Money

arly on in our marriage, I repeatedly said to Frank, "We're going to buy a house."

"No we're not."

"Yes we are."

"But when you go into debt people 'own' you," he insisted. In poverty, because the interest rates people pay are so high, they seemingly can never get them paid off.

"No they don't," I replied. "My parents were in debt for 30 years on their farm and they're not 'owned.'" They had a reasonable mortgage rate.

So we argued for a year. Then we found a house that was part of an estate sale. This was during the recession of the 1970s. Our combined income was $36,000 a year. We owed only $150 a month on our truck, so we weren't even close to the acceptable upper limit for indebtedness. The house payment was going to be just $300 a month. To my middle-class way of thinking, it was a good deal.

When we told Frank's mother we were buying a house, Mommy nearly had a heart attack. She went around telling everybody, "They're going to lose that house, they're going to lose that house— and then they're going to have to move in with one of us!" The real fear, of course, was that she would have to take us in.

So I kept repeating, "We are *not* going to lose this house." We bought it.

A year later we sold that house for 60 percent more than we had paid. Then everyone in Frank's family went out and bought a house. We thought that was great.

The Role of Abstractions, Paper, and Records

Imagine that your husband is killed in an accident. You receive a $6 million settlement. The pastor of your church encourages you to put the money in the bank and live off the interest. You put part of the interest back into the principal and receive an income of $5,000 a month (after taxes). All your relatives come to you and say that you must share. You explain that you can't because then you wouldn't get any money. They ask how much you're getting, so you tell them. They laugh and laugh, telling you "the man" (the banker) took everything, leaving you with next to nothing. He sends you a little bit each month to keep you quiet. You show them the bank statement. They laugh and laugh, saying anyone can put anything on paper. So you all go to the bank and ask to see the $6 million in the vault. Now the banker laughs.

Your husband is killed in an accident. You receive a $6 million settlement. You understand immediately that the Internal Revenue Service will get 40 percent, so you go to an accountant who gives you the name of a financial planner. Together you come up with a long-term financial plan. You pay off your current debts and put the rest of the settlement into a money market, index funds, and the stock market—in a conservative portfolio. You also probate your will upon the death of your spouse and get the legal paperwork changed to reflect your ownership.

Your husband is killed in an accident. His trust specifies the distribution of his assets. Your attorney works with the insurance company so that the payout of the $6 million occurs over six years, thereby minimizing the taxes. Further, you stipulate that the payout will go directly to your trust. You know you can "gift" up to $12,000 a year, so you gift off part of the $6 million each year to the trusts of your children. Your attorney handles the legal paperwork for the transfer of assets as the trust stipulates.

Explanation

To survive in poverty, you learn that your key sources of information are sensory and nonverbal. Your ability to react keeps you safe, so you rarely do any planning. Depending on your level of education, you may be less than comfortable reading, writing, and doing math.

To operate in the middle-class world, you must be able to handle paperwork and computerized records. Abstract representational systems are used for everything. For example, a checking account represents cash. A calendar represents time.

In wealth the abstract representations are for systemic issues over time. For example, a trust indicates how assets will be transferred over several generations. Holding companies are representational systems that bind multiple corporations together legally. In order to cope, you need expert counsel.

Interestingly, a common middle-class misunderstanding is that when you put money in the bank, it stays there. Actually, the cash is invested. In wealth, people see their financial accounts vary anywhere from $40,000 to millions a month, depending on how the investments are fluctuating. They understand that money management is about risk management.

In establishing my consulting company, we've all worked through the issue that you can't pay attention after a certain point to the amount of money that something costs. Rather you pay attention to the percentage of your gross income that it costs. Percentage is more significant than the exact amount. That was a hard transition for Frank. I must have worked with him for three years on that one concept.

He would go into orbit: "You're buying another computer!"

"Yes I am."

"But damn it, you just bought one."

"I did. But it's still only one-half percent of our overhead costs. So give it up."

I had to learn this stuff too, but it was initially easier for me than him because of my middle-class upbringing. Moving from poverty into wealth is a tough transition, which, as noted earlier, is part of the charm of the movie *Pretty Woman* where a *two*-class gap is being dealt with. Bottom line? In time Frank was OK with this strategy.

On the flip side, he kept me grounded. When the stock market was going up and up and up in the '90s, I kept saying, "We've got to invest, we've got to invest." Frank would said, "Ruby, it's a bubble, and it's going to bust."

So he kept me sane. He dragged his feet, and we argued more about investments than anything else in those years. But Frank wouldn't budge. In the end, when the market tanked in 2000, we lost less than 10 percent of our assets. Lots of people would have been grateful, as many lost half their assets. Because of Frank's knowledge about the stock market from working six years at the Chicago Board of Trade — and because of the skepticism about money that he had gotten honestly from growing up in poverty — my husband saved us a bundle.

In *Your* Life . . .

If you're moving from poverty into middle class, develop a simple system for tracking your paperwork. This is a must. Further, understand how important keeping track of paper is for survival in middle class. One of the men in poverty I know paid his wife child support in cash every Friday night for six years. Because of a rumor he spread about her (that happened to be true), she took him back to court. Because he had no written records, the court ordered him to pay another $10,000 in child support to her that he had already paid. He just couldn't prove it.

In addition, it will be important to honor the abstract frames of time and planning. Swallow your pride and learn to use a day planner or a schedule book. Get to meetings on time by using a clock, as opposed to what time it "feels like."

If you're in middle class and marry or move into the world of poverty, expect that there will be almost no pictures and few written records of anything. Scrapbooks, photo albums, wedding records, and the like will be virtually nonexistent. A few family pictures will be on the walls. But it isn't unusual that dates of death of family members can't be remembered and aren't recorded. Systems for keeping track of legal paperwork don't exist. Your spouse/partner will likely be careless about paper records and not understand the significance of them.

If you're moving from middle class into wealth, understand that paper documents are used to represent systems and things. Detailed records are kept of events, personal histories, possessions, and so forth because of the historical and artistic significance. For example, it isn't unusual that pictures are kept of all your catalogued designer clothing/shoes. There are simply too many to remember. Their location is catalogued as well. Jewelry, furniture, artwork, and cars are likewise catalogued. Advanced systems are used to keep track of such items as trusts and legal paperwork.

Three Typical Scenarios

Your spouse/partner has just told you he took the rent money to bail his brother out of jail. This is the third time this year it has happened, and you were promised it wouldn't happen again. In addition, the insurance has lapsed on the car and you don't know how that will get paid. And, last but not least, his brother was driving your spouse/partner's car, and his brother has no driver's license. The current discussion revolves around what to do about the bills, where the rent money will come from, and even how to get insurance again if there were money.

Your spouse/partner tells you the car insurance bill is 33 percent higher than it was last year, even though you have had no tickets or accidents. You spend three hours on the phone checking for lower premiums. You don't really want to take the time, but at present you have more time than money. The question is whether to change the deductible to a larger amount in order to lower the premium.

You and your spouse/partner are deciding whether to insure all your jewelry. Insurance is $2.50 per $100 of valuation, and you know it would cost you $25,000 to insure your jewelry. You're hesitant to insure it, not because of the expense, but because you know that thieves regularly find ways to peruse insurance policy addendums for such items as jewelry, original art, antiques, vintage cars, and furs. The discussion is about whether or not to insure it all, which portion of it, and the current security features in your three homes. Replacing the jewelry out of your own pocket wouldn't be a problem; it's simply how to position your assets so that all risks are minimized.

Explanation

In generational poverty, money is spent, and people are possessions. So when you get money, you spend it and share it with your friends. By the same token, when your friends have money, they share it with you. To withhold money from a friend or relative is to break the relationship. The hidden rule about money in poverty is: *If you have any money, and I ask for some, you share.*

Also in generational poverty there are virtually no wills or trusts. Possession is nine-tenths of the law. Whoever gets to an item first . . . it's theirs, unless there's a fistfight. At the same time, generational poverty is not so much about money; it's a state of mind. People in the culture of survival who suddenly come into a substantial sum of money seldom keep it very long. They give it to family and friends, they spend it quickly on big-ticket items, or they blow it on a merry-go-round of nonstop partying.

There are two main monetary issues in poverty. The first is that you don't properly manage what you have. The other is that you don't have enough.

Middle-class people think there's a 30-day rule about money before you get in trouble. Actually, it's a 90-day rule. For instance, with rental property, you pay your rent and a deposit, then you don't have to pay again. Rent counts for the first month you live somewhere. The deposit ends up counting for the second month. And when your landlord begins proceedings to evict you through the courts, it usually takes another month because judges don't want to evict without evidence of non-payment, as opposed to being late. That's a 90-day cycle. Legally you have to miss three house payments before the bank takes your house away from you. This is the same reason that many major corporations don't pay their bills until the 90th day after receiving an invoice.

In poverty, when there's not enough money, you might rotate paying bills. If you pay a bill this month, you might not pay it again for at least 60 days. It's always on a rotating basis. Utilities. Transportation. Childcare. Medicine. Clothing.

In middle class, money is used to build material security, and things (not people) are possessions. Middle-class folks use money to purchase liabilities, which over time become assets. For example, a home mortgage is a liability, but the home itself becomes an asset once it's paid off. Middle-class individuals purchase items that are solid, have value, and will last (at least) until they're paid for. The hidden rule about money in middle class: *I don't ask you for money, and you don't ask me.*

Middle-class folks have wills. A will indicates how things will be divvied up and transferred at the death of an individual. Wills typically address one generation.

In wealth, money is used to enhance social, financial, or political connections—and a possession in wealth generally is a one-of-a-kind object, a legacy, a bloodline, or an original work of art. Money is to be conserved and used for the building of additional wealth. There's an entire industry in the United States, headed by banks and investment firms, called wealth management/enhancement. What distinguishes the wealthy from the merely well-to-do are the bloodlines, the beauty, and the artistic quality of everything. The private boarding school, with its emphasis on excellence, also enters the mix.

When objects are purchased by the affluent, they come with provenance, a valuable piece of paper described in Chapter 7. Also in wealth there are trusts. A trust indicates how assets will be passed on from generation to generation. It is the systematic transfer of wealth over time.

Is there an exact number by which one crosses the line into wealth? Statistics show that if you have a household income of $200,000 or more you are in the top 2 percent of households in America. But there's skewed data about wealth in America. Only 2 to 2½ percent of households have a net worth of a million dollars or more. Since there are about 111 million households in America, 2 percent means 2 million households.

Bottom line: When your income is more than a million dollars, you lose all your income-tax deductions. So then you're really thrust into a category where you have to preserve wealth. At that level, money management is about protection.

One of the biggest issues in wealth is who to entrust with handling your money. You have dozens of accounts. You could be stripped of your wealth and literally not know it for months (recall the story of the Brazilian tycoon in Chapter 1). Tied in with the issue of one-of-a-kind objects is the issue of security and insurance. How do you protect assets? The hidden rule about money in wealth: *You don't talk about money* per se. *Investments yes, money no.*

In *Your* Life …

If you grew up in poverty and are moving into middle class, an issue you're likely to face will be sharing money with relatives and friends. The expectation is that you will share. Because you have the only car that starts in the winter, the expectation is that you will give them rides and jumpstart their cars. You'll have individuals tell you that you "owe" them because you made it out and they didn't. You're considered "lucky." It will be hard—and you will get resistance—but you must say, "We need to keep this money for our children."

A woman who made it out of poverty told me of going to bed at night and crying because she could no longer share her money with her extended family. She finally told herself, "I have to have the money. Somebody has to make it out. Otherwise, none of us will make it." Sometimes this is termed "lifeboat ethics." If too many people climb aboard a lifeboat, the boat sinks—and everyone is sunk.

Additionally, in the transition from poverty to middle class, it's important to recognize the role of credit and credit history. As noted above, middle-class folks have liabilities that, over time, become assets when they're completely paid. To create assets over time, credit

becomes vitally important. Bills must be paid in a timely fashion—
or the credit history will be negative.

If you're from middle class and marry into wealth, understand
that purchases will reflect an aesthetic sense and top-of-the-line
quality. To buy items that are commonly available would not be
acceptable. Also in wealth, items of value and merit come with
provenance, as noted above.

No matter what economic class you come from or marry into—
your class of origin or another—it's also important to remember:
If one person is almost always the giver, and the other is almost
always the taker, eventually both sides come to resent each other.

Where Your Disposable Income Goes

You spent your income-tax refund on a four-wheeler. You love that
four-wheeler. You traded your old pickup truck for a trailer and got
a new pickup on payments so you can haul your four-wheeler.

Your partner has just purchased a new set of golf clubs for you.
For your birthday, you bought yourself season tickets to the theater.
You gave your partner season tickets for his favorite college football
team.

You just spent $100,000 on a small sailboat and were lucky to get
a slip at the marina. You've been invited to be a member of the
Yacht Club ($15,000 initial fee), with monthly fees as well. You're
planning to sail in the annual regatta this fall.

You're on a corporate board. When you arrive at a meeting, the
car you're driving has a problem, and you must have it repaired.
One of the other board members offers the loan of a car. He takes you
to his garage where there are nine cars—a Rolls Royce, a Mercedes,
a couple of Lamborghinis, and a Porsche, among others. The butler
hands you a key and asks you to select a car. You protest and say,
"Shouldn't I pick a car before I get a key?" The butler tells you that
all the cars are coded to the same key, so one always has a choice.
Your car isn't repaired by the time the board meeting is over. The
other board member has you drive the borrowed car to your home.

A few days later he has an employee drive your car to you and pick his up.

Explanation

"Toys"—what you do with your leisure time and money—vary by gender. But they vary also by class because the activities around toys indicate your social set.

In poverty, things that can be done inexpensively (these can also be done more lavishly)—such as fishing, bowling, ballgames, dirt-track auto racing—are often the activities of choice. There's little money in the household, and the extra cash for toys usually goes to the men.

Statistics indicate that Americans living in poverty typically spend 50 to 60 percent of their gross income on housing. Middle-class folks spend 25 to 30 percent of their income on housing. What percentage do you think the wealthy spend? It's between 3 and 11 percent. Housing has a huge impact on disposable income.

My friend Kim shares how her family vacations now compare with those in her childhood.

> Both my parents came from the working poor. My parents gave me a foundation of work and financial security. All the personal resources were present, except money. Although there was only a small amount of disposable income, we were always comfortable and had a good home, not a fancy one. It was a small, two-bedroom house in a working-class neighborhood. My parents followed the middle-class rules. I remember Dad paying bills at the kitchen table and Mom pacing the floor trying to find a way to save a little something for a summer vacation.
>
> Every summer they'd put the tent in the back of the station wagon. We drove until we were half out of cash, then we'd turn around and come home. This is how I saw 27 or 28 states by the time I was 18. Our longest trip was to Michigan from Oklahoma. We went from Florida across Tennessee. We went to D.C. once—

also Colorado, New Mexico, and even a trip to the Grand Canyon. For that trip we pulled a camper behind the car.

As an adult, my attitudes haven't changed much. We're conservative spenders. We've always preferred to go places instead of buy things. But we take better vacations now. Instead of camping at the lake, we fly to a beach somewhere. We sent our kids to school where they wanted to go, but we still live in a relatively small house.

In middle class, toys tend to be a shared social activity—golf, driving snowmobiles, season tickets, and so on.

In wealth, because both money and opportunity are present, there's a veritable smorgasbord of choices in toys and activities.

Part of the issue in moving from one class to another is that some toys are more expensive than others, and learning to use them requires both money and lessons. For example, sailing is often found in wealth. (To get the total experience of sailing, stand in a cold shower and tear up hundred-dollar bills!) So unless you have had exposure to someone who has access to these toys, you won't know how to use them.

In *Your* Life ...

If you're moving from poverty to middle class, chances are you've worked so hard that you've had little time for leisure and sports—and little money for toys. If toys are purchased, they're often items that you're familiar with: four-wheelers (you already know how to drive), fishing gear, and the like. Sports tend to be those based on being a spectator, such as football, basketball, baseball, and auto racing, rather than participating. With the exception of auto racing, sports that are followed usually were played in public school.

If you're from middle class and marry into poverty, expect that toys will be an area of contention in your relationship, particularly the amount of money spent on activities. Both you and your partner likely will misunderstand and disapprove of each other's toys. Even though you learned some sports and activities without lessons, most of them (such as Little League baseball or youth soccer) still took time and cost money.

Expect that your spouse will not have had many of the experiences *or* lessons to be able to join you in what you enjoy … and likely won't want to take lessons as an adult. Also recognize up front that some of the activities your husband engages in—such as riding all-terrain vehicles over the countryside, shooting rabbits and other wildlife, and gambling while playing poker and pool with the boys at the bar two or three nights a week—will seem inappropriate to you.

If you're moving from middle class to wealth, it will be important to take lessons in tennis, golf, sailing, or exotic sports like scuba diving, sky diving, and hot-air ballooning. Many social connections are made or enhanced through sporting events.

What is clearly understood in old wealth is that the connections, particularly the international ones, will make or break the family assets over time. Assets are moved around internationally, depending on the political situations in different countries (wars, economic disasters, military coups, and so forth). Your connections give you advance warning—and also the tools with which to move the assets.

CHAPTER 12
Your Social Activities, Friends, and Connections

About 25 years ago Frank needed to speak to one of the guys in his old neighborhood. We lived near the neighborhood for eight years, so it was easy to stop by. It was a summer evening, and the men were outdoors, standing and sitting under a tree in a circle drinking beer. (If you've seen the TV show "King of the Hill," it was a little like that, you know, where Hank and his male buddies are hanging out at the fence.) This is common in low-income neighborhoods. They were telling stories about their work, their fights, and their sexual encounters. I've eavesdropped, so I know. That night, there was howling coming out of the tree. When I looked up, I could see a middle-aged white man in the branches, howling, and I didn't think this was normal.

"What's wrong with him?" I asked.

They all laughed and finally one said, "Ain't nothin' wrong with him, Ruby, except he's up in that tree. He thinks he's Tarzan, and he's huntin' for Jane." In poverty a wider range of behaviors is acceptable than in middle class.

I was not easily dissuaded. "No, there's something wrong with that man. We need to bring him *down*."

Oh, they laughed and laughed and laughed. Finally another one said, "Ruby, ain't nothin' wrong with him except that he's drunk."

"That's even worse," I replied. "What if he falls out of the tree and hurts himself?"

They laughed some more. "Well, Ruby, I reckon he won't be climbin' that tree drunk no more, now will he?"

I couldn't let it alone. "We've got to call the police department. We've got to get the fire department out here. We've got to get that man out of that tree!"

My concern for this man's welfare seemed to be the greatest amusement they'd ever had, they laughed so hard. "Ruby, leave him alone," one of them told me. "He ain't hurtin' nobody. Besides, he might get lucky and find Jane." So they left the man up in the tree all night. I know, because he woke me up at 3 a.m., howling. I could hear him from two blocks away. About noon the next day, he came down.

If it had been a middle-class neighborhood, you can rest assured the police and fire department would've been called. We would've had an ambulance out there. We would pay someone to shoot him with tranquilizer darts. We'd be there with a big net under the tree, waiting to catch him when he keeled over. Then when the incident was over, we would hold a meeting of the Neighborhood Association to put a new rule in the bylaws: "No howling from trees in this neighborhood!"

Interestingly, middle-class people—not unlike those in poverty—tolerate a wider range of behaviors than the affluent. Once I was at a party among wealthy women and they laughed for ten minutes about a man who wore a sweater to the country club to go golfing. I never did fully understand the joke, but I think it had to do with the fact that you're supposed to wear a shirt on the golf course.

Frank took a lot of heat in his old neighborhood for marrying me. One time somebody said to him in front of me, "You need to send that girl back to school for a class in obedience." I thought he handled this comment pretty well, considering he was in a difficult place. He said, "Well, she's already flunked twice. I doubt it would do any good."

Do any of three following scenarios seem familiar to you?

Typical Scenarios

You worked hard this week, and now it's Friday night. Your wife/companion and kids are at home. You meet your buddies at the local bar where you cash your check and buy your buddies a round of drinks. You play some pool. You "trash talk" for a while, trading stories about work, fights, sports, and sex. It's getting later. Your wife calls the bar looking for you, but you tell the bartender to tell her you aren't there. You know there's going to be hell to pay and a big fight tomorrow about what you're doing, so you just stay at the bar until it closes.

You've worked hard this week and it's Friday night. You and your spouse/partner have made plans to go out to dinner with mutual friends. Yesterday afternoon you went to a soccer game your daughter was involved in, then later a Little League game involving your son. Wednesday evening you had a church meeting. Tonight you hired a baby sitter for your children. Your paycheck and that of your spouse/partner were electronically deposited into your bank account. You'll pay most of your bills online tomorrow. Your spouse/partner made the reservation at the restaurant for your evening out.

It's Friday night, and you and your spouse/partner have tickets to attend an art opening, which you'll follow with a late dinner. A portion of the proceeds from the art opening will be donated to AIDS research. While you don't particularly care for this artist, you know that several contacts can be made there with individuals who may support your literacy charity later in the year. The nanny has the children. Your administrative assistant at the office reserved a table in your name at a five-star restaurant.

Explanation

Socializing in poverty is generally a separate event for men and women. Even when attending the same event, males usually socialize with males and females with females. Rarely will a couple go out alone.

Humor is a big component of socializing in poverty. Frank's family would sit around on the porch thinking up one-liners to top each other. To jokingly insult someone's intelligence, for instance, Mommy would make feisty, acerbic comments like: "She's got all the buttons, but the threads are loose" and "You could piss in the air, and she'd think it was raining."

In middle class, shopping trips, "ladies' nights out," fishing trips, and golf dates are all opportunities for socialization with the same gender. When couples attend a social event, they generally spend some of the time together, some of the time apart. Some socialization is strictly for the couple, such as dinners, movies, and celebrations of an anniversary or promotion.

In wealth, socialization is often for the general purpose of net-working—making new connections and strengthening old ones—and for finding ways to generate support for your favorite causes.

Among all groups and classes, to be sure, socialization also is simply about spending time with friends.

In *Your* Life ...

A big issue in socializing is: What do you talk about? Conversation tends to come from shared experience and shared understandings.

If you're from poverty and marry into middle class, you'll need to develop a comfort level with mixed-gender socializing that does *not* have an ulterior sexual motive. You'll need to find topics to talk about with the opposite sex (and, to a lesser degree, with your own gender) that are "acceptable." These conversations could include sports, your children and their activities, incidents at work (but nothing particularly derogatory about individuals), current events, church, or club activities. Especially with the opposite sex, these conversations would *not* include sexual, racist, or sexist jokes. You also will want to steer clear of starting an argument that becomes physical or having a display of jealousy about your spouse/significant other.

I know of a man who got a divorce essentially because his wife couldn't make the climb from poverty to middle class. It was an issue of mindset. She believed that if her husband got promoted he would leave her, and this scared her greatly. As we've seen elsewhere, the poverty mindset was that he was her possession. To prevent the loss from happening, she called his bosses and chewed them out behind his back. Several months later her worst fear was realized; he divorced her.

If you're from middle class and marry into poverty, expect that you and your spouse will lead parallel lives socially. Your spouse/ partner will be uncomfortable with the middle-class concepts of socializing and won't know what to talk about that would be acceptable. Expect that he/she will be jealous of your friends if you spend too much time with them. Expect that work situations that involve you and a person of the opposite sex will be very difficult for your spouse/significant other to accept. Expect also that your spouse/ partner will be uncomfortable with the socializing "dress code" used in middle class.

If you're from middle class and marry into wealth, expect that a great deal of socializing will deal with charitable causes, art shows, and business networking. Appropriate dress will be required. Conversations will center on whom you know (your connections) and where you've traveled. In addition, conversations will revolve around the boards you're on; developments in the worlds of art and fashion; and sporting events, such as golf, tennis, sailing, and skiing (both as a participant and a spectator).

As you climb the economic ladder, expertise becomes more and more valued, as you eventually can afford whatever you need — indeed, whatever you want. What distinguishes the way you live are the quality, artistic flair, and aesthetic appeal of your situation. To make such determinations, you need expertise.

If you marry into wealth, understand the importance of this. In fact, expertise around wine is often used as a "test." A middle-class friend of mine, John, was dating a wealthy woman. The first time John went out to dinner with her friends, one of them said to John, "Why don't you select the wine?" He understood immediately that it was a test to see if he "fit." It happens that he is a connoisseur of wine and made the correct selection. John told me later, "The most expensive wine is not necessarily the best, nor are the best-known names. The year also is important." So in particular, educate yourself about wines and artists. Those are two vital areas of expertise.

If you're from middle class and marry into wealth, as we've seen in earlier chapters, don't introduce yourself at social events. I have made this mistake. Basically, if you do, people just turn around and walk off. They won't say a word to you. Wait to be introduced. If this hidden rule seems odd to you, be assured that if you were wealthy you would do the same thing. Put yourself in their shoes. Suppose you were at a party, and I came up and introduced myself to you. You would be thinking, "Who is she and what does she want? If she were anybody significant, I would have been introduced to her."

When you *are* introduced, your connection will be stated: "This is so-and-so with such-and-such firm or family." Remember, a possession is a one-of-a-kind object. This includes your pedigree or a bloodline, which is literally something that no one else can have. If they were to say, "This is Ruby, and she's my *very dear friend*," it means they like me, but I have no significant associations.

To introduce yourself to someone is to immediately announce that you are middle class. Moreover, you won't be forgiven if you abuse a connection by making a comment such as, "So-and-so suggested I come talk to you."

If you're from wealth and marry into middle class, understand that *not* introducing yourself at a social gathering likely would be considered snobbish.

The Role of Respect

You're traveling on a two-lane highway with your husband and his brother. You're driving, and the driver behind you (a sport utility vehicle full of college students) is riding your bumper. Finally, you pull over because it's dangerous and let the SUV go around you. One of the college kids sticks his head out the window and yells, "Park that piece of s---." You raise an eyebrow and get back on the highway. About ten miles down the road, you stop for gas. Unbeknownst to you, the SUV also has stopped—at a restaurant behind the gas station. You get gas and are ready to start the car. Your husband angrily says to you, "Want me to go teach those guys in the SUV a lesson? They had no right to talk to you that way!" And his brother adds, "Yeah, I carry a pocketknife for jerks like that!"

You're traveling at the speed limit on a six-lane interstate. The guy behind you has been riding your bumper. You decide he's an idiot and, as soon as possible, move into another lane. As he passes you, he rolls down his window and gives you the finger. You ignore him and continue carefully driving. You're too busy thinking about work and what you need to get finished today to be upset by another driver.

You're double-parked in an exclusive area of town, waiting for your spouse. Just as your spouse gets in the car, a Bentley swings in front of you, blocking you from leaving. You honk at the driver of the Bentley, gesturing for him to move. He does nothing, not even acknowledging you. You are livid. You get out and bang on his trunk, yelling at him to move up a bit so you can get out. He grudgingly does so. Ten minutes later you're pulled over by a city police officer and receive a $100 ticket for double parking. You understand exactly what has occurred.

Explanation

In poverty you aren't respected unless you're personally strong. What is greatly respected is physical strength. While "book smarts" may be tolerated, they aren't respected.

In middle class, respect corresponds with the level of achievement or position a person has attained. Position and achievement represent a level of stability and material security.

Among the affluent, as we've seen earlier, respect is earned through artistry, expertise, and connections. It also is associated with privilege. While every class has a concept of privilege, in wealth the hidden rule is: "I have enough connections and enough money to make the system work for me. I know how to do that." The wealthy use the resources of the community to handle conflicts. So if they feel threatened by something (such as someone banging on a Bentley), they call the police and expect action to be taken promptly. There also may be a sense that "the rules do not apply to me; I will manipulate the system so I can have my way."

In *Your* Life . . .

If you're from middle class and marry into poverty, understand the need of your spouse or partner to defend you. In a variety of social settings, he/she will do an "in your face" on your behalf.

If you're from poverty and move into middle class, understand that displays of physical strength are not respected in middle class. In fact, they're frowned upon. To physically fight with someone over an issue rather than work it out through discussion is considered unsophisticated and not in control ("Physical force is the last refuge of little minds").

If you're from middle class and marry into wealth, understand the importance to your spouse of networking and having the proper associations, as well as the underlying need for security. Your spouse probably will not handle interpersonal conflicts directly but instead will use public and private intermediaries, such as police, bodyguards, lawyers, and the like.

CHAPTER 13

How You Approach Religion and Charity

*Y*ou go to the Gospel Mission Church every Sunday. The congregation is small and meets for several hours on Sunday morning, with services sometimes extending into early afternoon. It is evangelical and evangelistic, with an altar call almost every Sunday morning. The preacher considers himself (yes, the minister is male) a friend of God and preaches from the heart. He has had little or no theological training. He lives in the house next to the church building that the congregation bought. Neither he nor his wife works outside the ministry. Both drive used Cadillacs. The offerings are taken every Sunday and collected by the preacher. There are no written records of the offerings. You give a lot of your money to the church because the preacher and his wife have been so good to you. In fact, when you sell your house, they ask you to give part of the money to the church. Your congregation is an independent Bible-believing church.

You go to the United Methodist Church where you are a deacon. There are two services on Sunday morning: an early service and a late service. Sunday school is sandwiched between the two. No service lasts longer than an hour. On the rare occasions it starts going past an hour, people begin looking at their watch in not-so-subtle ways. The pastor is full-time, and it's a paid position. Written budgets are provided to church members, and tithes are strongly encouraged as a part of membership. Worship services and other meetings are planned several months in advance. Written materials used in Sunday school are purchased from a religious publishing company and provided to members at no cost. Your congregation is a part of a larger conference of churches.

You go to the First Presbyterian Church. You don't attend every Sunday. Your family donated the organ to the church and has a long history of membership. You're part of a group that has worked very hard to set up an endowment for the church and its ministry. The ministers, choir director, and organist have doctorates in their respective area of expertise.

Explanation

First, it should be noted that organized religion serves a variety of purposes for people in every class. For some, organized religion serves a spiritual purpose, for some it's more of a social purpose, for some it's a way to give back to the community, and for some it offers resources and solace. Its purpose can be a combination of any or all of these.

"When my wife and I were getting out of poverty, we had our family and our faith," says one man. "It was the spiritual piece that turned the situation around. We knew that was a resource we could hold onto when I was in school. We were alone in the big city and didn't live near our parents. In time, through the church, we came to have more support systems, as several people befriended us."

In poverty, religion is viewed largely as the female's responsibility. The mother tends to be "keeper of the soul"; she dispenses forgiveness and punishment. Spiritual beliefs are instilled at a young age. By the time children are pre-teens, it's expected that they can choose. Men in poverty typically don't attend church unless they're in a leadership role (minister, deacon, song leader, or the like). If the mother doesn't take part in religious activities, chances are good that no one else in the household will either. The church provides a support system and resources. One woman who has made the transition, with her husband, from poverty to middle class has this to say about finances and the church.

He probably would give more to the church than I would, because he doesn't know as much about the checkbook I do. If he's got a hundred dollars in his pocket, he's fine. For sure, he would give away his hundred dollars anytime. In Sunday school he heard about tithing, but he doesn't know what we actually do or don't do. One of these days he may say, "Open up that checkbook, Honey, and let me take a look."

Of course, it puts a huge burden on me. I've tried occasionally to look at it with him. But he just doesn't seem to care. We don't fight about money. Maybe we should.

In middle class, religion is usually a joint decision. However, it isn't unusual for spouses or partners to attend different churches. For example, one spouse may be Catholic and the other Protestant. Or one may be Jewish and the other Protestant. Religion also provides an opportunity for social networking in middle class.

In wealth, as in the other classes, organized religion serves individuals in a variety of ways. But in wealth it's frequently also seen and used as a way to give back to the community. It becomes a charitable organization in its own right. In old money it may be a way of enhancing a personal legacy as well—for instance, through large financial contributions to a new church wing, a pipe organ, and so forth.

In *Your* Life . . .

In poverty, if a woman is a devout church attendee, you can expect that she'll likely stay in an abusive domestic situation because it's considered "the will of God" (or Allah) to do so. After all, the Bible and the Quran say the wife must submit to her husband. Many prayers at the church or mosque will be said for her. She will serve as a "holy witness" in her willingness to keep submitting to her abusive husband, who sometimes also raises his hand against the children. If you try to get such a woman to leave an abusive situation, it's important to talk to her about the safety of her children (not just her personal safety) and about being a good mother.

Expect that a disproportionate amount of money in poverty will be given to the church/mosque and that the money will not be accounted for. Also understand that the beliefs expressed tend to be *very* literal to the written text of the Bible or Quran, and interpretations of religious text will be made with little or no contextual or cultural understanding. Expect that the beliefs expressed will have idiosyncratic applications that are dependent on the interpretations of the leadership of the church or mosque. Occasionally, specific individuals will be mentioned during the sermon and held up for public censure or condemnation.

In middle class assume that families who attend church will give a great deal of time to church activities. Church is viewed as a good source of support when you have children. The church activities are good for children and keep them on the "right path." It should be noted that some middle-class congregations are hotbeds of gossip, intrigue, and backbiting. People making the transition from poverty to middle class are sometimes stunned by the amount of that sort of mean-spirited activity, then are disillusioned and quit going to church. If you're from poverty and moving into a middle-class church, appearances also are important.

In wealth someone who is well-educated does the interpretation of the religious text, and the interpretation will be almost secular in its application. Right and wrong tend to be interpreted contextually and "relatively" at an individual level and are rarely applied to everyone. The larger framework of cultural variations, religious interpretation, and personal meaning are examined from a national or global perspective.

Some Hidden Rules of Charity

Your friend asks you for money. You "spot" him some. But at work, they have a big meeting about the United Way and how much everyone is supposed to give. You don't know anybody who gives to a charity because most of the people you know don't trust those charities, plus they don't have extra money growing on trees. But you sign up to give $10 a week to see how it works. Your boss comes back to your work area and tells you ten bucks isn't enough. You tell him to kiss your a--, then add for good measure that you aren't giving *anything* to United Way. Driving home, you've cooled off a bit and think of something else you could've said to your boss: Your spouse/partner goes to church, and a lot of money is given there. After all, God is your friend, and it's important to share.

Your friend asks you for money. You're stunned, but you explain that you don't have any right now. But at work they have a big meeting about the United Way and how much everyone is supposed to give. On the form you check the amount suggested because you know your boss is watching—and that raising a certain amount of money is a company goal. You know promotions are linked to "playing ball" with management in such matters. At the church you attend, you and your spouse/partner give between 5 percent and 10 percent of your income. You also volunteer to coordinate and collect some of the donations for the United Way.

Your friend asks you to invest in a bank he is starting. These are private shares, and they aren't insured. There's a chance of an excellent return, but it's also very high-risk. You aren't sure you trust him. In essence, it's a totally unsecured loan—practically a gift. You're on the board of directors for the United Way, but you give the majority of your money to charity through your own non-profit foundation, which you established to fund the causes in which you're interested. You donate your time on the boards of several other charities and participate socially in their fund-raising events. Because only 5 percent of the proceeds from the charity must be used for that particular cause, you use the funds to host fund-raisers, and that takes a great deal of time. You like functioning at the policy-making and decision-making level.

Explanation

In poverty very rarely are time or money given to anonymous charities. Money and help are given to friends or relatives—not to people you don't know. As a matter of fact, there's a great deal of distrust about charities. The strong feeling is that most of the money doesn't go to help individuals in need but instead lines the pockets of the people who work for the charities. Also, in poverty you know at least one person who has some kind of donation scam going. Things no longer used or worn are often thrown away—or stored, pack rat–style, in cluttered piles and in closets.

In middle class much time (as well as money) is given to charities and causes. Donations of clothing, food, books, and other items provide a convenient way of discarding things while serving a worthy cause. Because purchases were made based on quality, things are given away rather than thrown away.

In wealth the role of charities is paramount, in part because of the way tax laws are written and in part due to the strong ethic of the privileged in society "giving back," sometimes called *noblesse oblige*. Charities also serve as the backbone of the social structure. Considerable time is given to the policy aspects of charities, such as serving on boards and going to planning meetings.

In *Your* Life . . .

If you're from middle class and marry into poverty, expect that your spouse/partner will have a great deal of difficulty accepting the amount of time and money you give to causes. Often his/her understanding of charity will be that it's a waste of time and money; it only makes the directors of the charities rich.

If you're from poverty and marry into middle class, expect that your spouse/significant other may have difficulty understanding the amount of money and time you give to help your friends. The middle-class assumption is that your friends should be self-sufficient and *plan ahead* for emergencies. Some of these feelings may also apply to family, especially extended family.

If you're from middle class and marry into wealth, expect that a great deal of time will be given to charities. In fact, if you're female, understand that you're expected to volunteer your time to charities and not to work (that is, get paid) at a job *per se*. Among the affluent, to work for money tends to be viewed as "common."

A colleague of mine describes the clash of her hidden rules with those of her spouse.

> *My husband is in a service club with many people I don't know, a middle- to upper-class group of people who are doctors and attorneys, as well as other professionals. He has met these people in the course of his business. It's a networking association that's focused on service. The meetings are always held at the country club. I'm not comfortable there. He joined the country club for us, so we'd have a place we can go and eat. But I hate that. I should be the one who likes it, but I don't. I'm probably too middle class to go and enjoy mixing and mingling. I'd rather be working.*
>
> *His impulse is to network. He enjoys it. But it's a transition I haven't made. If he were to make me feel bad, then it would strain our marriage. If he were to start going by himself, for example, it would bother me, and then I'd make a point to go. He hasn't done that. He's just having a good time and visiting. We do believe in giving—and more than we used to. His membership in this organization requires it.*

If you're from wealth and marry into middle class, recognize that your spouse won't understand the significance of belonging to exclusive organizations. In his book *Our Kind of People* (see Bibliography) on the African-American elite, journalist Lawrence Otis Graham quotes a middle-class professional: "'Why does the whole organization need to know what my husband and children do for a living?' asked the Los Angeles attorney, who admits she was surprised when she was passed over for membership into the group. 'They might as well list where our parents went to college. How is any of this relevant?'"

CHAPTER 14

Tips for Making the Transition from Poverty to Middle Class

*S*o you're making a transition from poverty to middle class. The trouble is you don't think like the people you grew up with anymore, yet you don't think like the people you're with now. It's a lonely place. And it's difficult to find people to trust. Who do you know who is like you? Very often . . . no one.

Good news. There are ways to smooth your transition and ensure that it lasts. Some of the tips in this chapter are ways that you can help yourself. Others are ways your significant other can help you. While these suggestions are rooted in an understanding of the hidden rules of class, they also incorporate the ten qualities of resilient people described in Chapter 2.

Let's begin by looking at your financial picture.

Make a Budget

Unless you learn to embrace the mindsets of middle class—such as planning, attention to detail, and accountability—you may find yourself reverting to poverty. Here's a worst-case scenario that highlights some typical mistakes.

You and your spouse were raised in poverty, and last year you made $60,000. You bought a house for $45,000, and it needs a lot of work, but it's a house. Although you don't have a budget, you and your spouse have paid it off by working hard and saving money. But then you get very involved in a church and give a lot of money to the church. You get behind on your utilities, and your husband gets drunk and wrecks the car. You are "upside down" on the car (you owe more than it is worth), and the car was underinsured, so that amount is added to your car payment. You get some money for your birthday, but rather than pay off the bill, you buy an iguana. Your husband leaves you. You're having difficulty making payments. You get a second mortgage. Within a year, you have lost your house and declared bankruptcy.

Middle-class people focus a great deal of attention on creating financial stability, which is generally achieved through diligent planning to manage future needs. To prepare for success, the tool you will need to learn to master is the *budget*. Essentially, this means creating a written document comparing your anticipated income and anticipated expenses on a weekly, monthly, and annual basis. When you write things down, they become concrete, rather than imagined.

Depending on your short-term goals (e.g., buy groceries, pay your utility bill, go to the dentist, fill up the gas tank, take a summer vacation) and your long-term goals (e.g., pay off your credit card debt, buy a house, save for your children's college tuition, save for retirement), your budget will enable you to balance your income and your expenses so the two figures come out equal.

You may discover that you have a *surplus* of income—meaning you have disposable income to do with as you please. Or you may discover that you have a *deficit* of income—meaning that you are overspending and cannot meet your needs. In the latter case, you need to do one of two things: reduce your expenses or increase your income.

Do you need help to create a realistic budget? Here are a few ideas for doing that:

■ Go to the library and check out a book on the subject.

■ Go online and research it.

■ Take an adult education course in your community.

- Find a role model or mentor. Ask your spouse, a knowledgeable friend, or a knowledgeable relative to guide you.

- Hire a bookkeeper to help you create a system.

- Track your actual daily expenses on paper for one entire month and see where you *really* spend your money.

Avoid Destructive Relationships and Self-Sabotage

One of the biggest issues you may have to deal with when you're making the climb out of poverty is the expectation of the people in your old neighborhood—friends as well as family—that you will give your money to them. Many people allow this hidden rule to prevent them from striving for greater prosperity.

My friend Becky had a foster daughter named Helen. When Helen turned 19, Becky said to her, "Helen, you've got one more class at the high school to take, and after that you'll have your diploma. Then you'll need to get a job."

Helen said, "Well, that would be dumb."

When Becky recovered, she said, "I don't understand."

Helen answered, "They'll just take it away from me."

"Now I'm really confused," said Becky. "Who is going to take what away from you?"

"My mom and my sisters. They'll take my money, so there's no point in working."

Helen was ready to simply give up. But you don't have to be so resigned or fatalistic. You'll need to come to a private peace with how to handle other people's expectations of you sharing your income with them. But it's critically important to understand that you have a choice. You can set manageable levels of sharing, thereby ensuring that you can afford it. (Review your budget!) You also can say no. Frank and I chose to donate money to a homeless shelter in his old neighborhood as a way of giving back.

You may fear angering people and losing relationships. You may feel sad or lonely. Your impulse may be to turn to alcohol, recreational drugs, overeating, impulse shopping, or excessive TV watching to escape from the pain you feel. These solutions are not healthy, as they don't remove the source of your pain in the long run. You have to deal with reality sooner or later, or greater problems may arise. Developing your emotional and spiritual resources will enable you to be more resilient in the face of grief and other emotional turbulence, as well as other stresses in this period of change.

What would help you feel more peaceful inside? Confide in your significant other or a friend. Seek professional counseling from a therapist or spiritual leader. Start keeping a journal of your intimate thoughts (for your eyes only). Learn to meditate. Walk in nature. Soak in a bubble bath. Listen to music you love. Exercise. Go dancing. Decide to let go and move on; you are not your feelings. Act as if you are your own best friend.

An educational consultant on my staff reports, "I carry my Bible with me all the time. It is my main spiritual resource. Usually I leave it in my hotel room, but I can remember one very stressful assignment where I felt I needed to read it every day on my lunch break. It was a real struggle. I recall that a young man walked into the conference room where I was sitting and was surprised. He said, 'Wow, you do that during the day. Are we that mean?' I reassured him: 'It's not about anyone being mean. It's about my staying peaceful and strong.' "

Seek Positive Role Models

"I was fortunate to have a person in my life, a music teacher, who educated me about the middle- and upper-class lifestyle," an acquaintance told me. "Her family was wealthy, and she took me 'under wing.' I didn't know it at the time, but she took me to *very* nice places; she exposed me only to *the best*. We went to concerts and theater, and as a result I knew that I wanted to work hard to improve my circumstances. I started working early in my life because

I could play music. As a musician, I made more money than most of the people I knew because I got jobs at funeral homes playing for the mourners. It took me more than one try to get through school. But I did it."

People can only do the things they can imagine. So it's vital to have role models whose measure you can use as a guideline for personal transformation. Take Michael, a young man from New York City who spoke with a strong street dialect from the Bronx neighborhood where he grew up. Hoping to get a better job, he purposely changed his accent by imitating the speech patterns of the newscasters on TV every night. After a few months, his former dialect was almost imperceptible. He also made a point of reading the dictionary and learning three new words every day. Today he is a confident speaker.

"I came from an educated family. I am in the fourth or fifth generation of college-educated people," says a middle-class woman of African-American descent. "My grandmother was a chef and cooked in someone's kitchen, but she had a college degree, and so did her mother. My mother and father both had master's degrees. I was the first in the family to get a doctorate. On my mother's side especially (no shock) three sisters and a brother were college-educated. Frankly, I never thought of doing anything else."

By way of comparison, her husband came from poverty. Nonetheless, his role models were equally significant. The woman continues: "My husband's parents worked in a gas station and a restaurant. His poverty cycle breaker came from his parents' exposure to a better lifestyle through seeing the lives of the people they served. They recognized that those people had educations, and they discussed this fact openly with their son. He was self-motivated. He also observed how other people lived, and he wanted to have his own business."

When you have relationships with one or more role models, the best thing you can do is ask them questions. For example:

- How did they get started doing what they do? (People love to talk about this.)

- On a day-in, day-out basis, how do they actually do what they now do?

- What steps are involved?

- In what sequence are the steps?

- How long does each step take to accomplish?

- What element or elements do they consider important or a priority?

- Is there anything in particular that helped him/her become better at doing what he/she does?

Role models can help you think through the various steps to your goals so you can make them a reality. They can point you in the right direction.

Learn the Hidden Rules

If you're making the transition from poverty to middle class, here are some of the mindsets and issues that will need to be addressed.

- You may have to be nice to people you don't like. Just because someone is a jerk doesn't mean you can tell him/her to "f--- off."

- Jokes and comments about sexual activities are not acceptable in the workplace or at middle-class social events.

- The reactive mindset necessary to survive in poverty is not respected in middle class. Being proactive (planning) *is* respected.

- People are not viewed as possessions in middle class. Things are.

- Things are *not* always shared in middle class. Money is seldom shared in middle class.

- The needs of your immediate family come well before the needs of your relatives.

- Your mother does *not* have more say-so in your life than your spouse.

- Physical threats and violence are not condoned. Do not physically threaten someone in middle class. Such threats are taken seriously.

- Being sexually active outside of marriage is not viewed as an asset in middle class. Indeed, it often is viewed as a liability, as it interferes with the stability of the family and health. Plus it carries legal ramifications.

- Crisis making, clutter, and confusion are frowned upon in middle class.

- It's expected that you will have an organizational system for legal and financial paperwork. Paper records and computerized files with backup systems are very important.

- To be an accomplished and constant entertainer or storyteller doesn't have the same value in middle class as it does in poverty.

- A real man in poverty stands up to his wife. A real man in middle class negotiates with his wife.

- Honoring time frames is essential in middle class.

Helping Your Spouse Make the Transition

If you're middle class and married to someone from poverty, here are some mindsets and issues that may need your attention.

- Expect that periodically you will pay to get your spouse's sibling out of jail. The sibling was at your spouse's "back" when he/she was growing up. Now it's payback time.

- The quantity of food in the house will be more than you consider necessary.

- Your spouse may be deceptive about little things that have very little significance. Part of the reality of poverty can be that you don't tell the truth about many things—because it wouldn't be understood. You say you have things when you don't.

- Don't be surprised if your spouse is very protective and comes strongly to your defense in the presence of a perceived threat.

- Understand that your spouse may be more pessimistic and fatalistic (rather than positive and proactive) about life than you are.

- You may need to get used to the TV being on, with the volume up, more than you would prefer.

- Expect that your spouse/partner's mother will receive a tremendous amount of his/her time and attention. You may be surprised to see your mother-in-law be manipulative of your spouse while playing favorites among her children.

- "Spare the rod and spoil the child" may be a favorite saying of your spouse. There might even be situations where you need to personally stand between your child and a belt being wielded by your spouse.

- Be prepared for many purchases of items that you consider much less important (even frivolous) when bigger, more urgent, bills are left unpaid. Also, if your spouse gets some kind of financial windfall, understand that there may be pressure simply to give most of it to relatives and friends who ask.

- Your spouse/partner's relatives (and now yours) will likely regale you and each other with story after story, many of which are bawdy and hilarious, but some of which may seem off-color and stereotypical to you. And you may be surprised (and disappointed) how little discretionary time your spouse spends with you compared with his/her friends and relatives from poverty.

- Psychologically prepare yourself for your spouse to hold a succession of jobs, some of which are quit over what seems like a petty dispute with the boss—even when the job has benefits and a good hourly wage.

- Learn to "go with the flow" regarding appointments and time frames. Simply put, your spouse will get there when he/she gets there—and not sooner. Except for punching in at work, living in the moment is not controlled by a clock.

A Few Thoughts on Emotional Safety

There may be things your spouse can't talk about from his/her experience of growing up poor. There are simply no words (in some ways like a veteran returning from war), because there is too much pain and shame.

A colleague explains how shame affected her. "When I was a kid it was a hidden rule not to talk about the bad things that happen. You can go to school and never tell anyone. I knew that you didn't. Otherwise, you could lose your parents, be taken away and put in a foster home—and you feared those things worse than what you went through at home. You feared the unknown and foster care because you'd heard bad stories. As an adult, I still never talk about those things. It just became a habit, I guess."

A middle-class woman whose husband grew up in poverty tells this story.

*We never spend holidays at his parents' house. We have in the
past, but we discovered it's not a good thing. They don't make a
big deal of holidays. When we got engaged, I was helping him
clean their house and we found packages stored away. I excitedly
said, "Look, they left you Christmas presents!"*

*"No," he told me, his face red, "in our family, we always give
gifts after Christmas." His parents waited for things to be on sale
and told the kids that way they got more. Those boxes were fake
presents they put under the tree. It broke my heart. The fake presents did me in. We don't speak about this. It's a touchy thing.*

Psychologist John Bradshaw says toxic shame is when we feel as
though having a genuine human need or a drive proves there is
something wrong with us. It has the sense of being flawed, defective,
or a mistake, and it's accompanied by the fear of abandonment
and rejection. In his book *Healing the Shame That Binds You* (see
Bibliography), Bradshaw writes, "The need to identify with someone, to feel a part of something, to belong somewhere, is one of our
most basic needs. With the exception of self-preservation, no other
striving is as compelling as this need, which begins with our care-
givers or significant others and extends to family, peer group, culture,
nation and world."

To create emotional safety, it's important to let your significant
other know that he/she is acceptable to you. Be respectful of any
need for privacy, while at the same time letting your spouse know
clearly that you are willing to listen without passing judgment. Be
nurturing and practice verbal appreciation. Your kind words can
begin to replace the negative and critical voices that still reverberate
in your spouse's head.

Encourage and Celebrate Achievement

Every community has a phrase for it. In poor white neighborhoods,
they'll say, "You're getting above your raisings. You're too big for
your britches. You're uppity." In poor African-American neighbor-

hoods, they often call the ones who make the transition to middle class Oreos. In poor Hispanic neighborhoods, they call them Coconuts. In poor Asian neighborhoods, they call them Bananas. In poor Native American neighborhoods, they call them Apples—red on the outside and white on the inside. But the issue is still the same: We're afraid we're going to lose you. As a result, education and achievement are subtly, and even openly, discouraged.

You can support your spouse to achieve by being truly interested in success in school or on the job. Spend five to ten minutes a day just talking and asking questions about his/her day:

- "Are you OK?"
- "Did you get your work done?"
- "Did you have enough to eat?"
- "Did you do your homework?"   •
- "Is there anything you need?"

Offer to help your significant other rehearse for social and work-related events that are outside his/her experience or expertise. Who will attend? What are the steps that will be followed? For the same reason that many athletes visualize their competition in advance, it's useful and relaxing to know ahead of time what will likely happen in new settings. Then you and your partner can be prepared for possible challenges. Create a mutual strategy for ongoing support at parties or family gatherings. Afterward have a discussion to make sure that you're both comfortable with what has happened. There's always a next time . . . Perhaps a different approach would be preferable?

Last, but not least: Lighten up. Remember why you love your spouse. Focus on those positive qualities. Maintain a sense of humor.

CHAPTER 15

Tips for Making the Transition from Middle Class to Wealth

As we saw in the last chapter, one of the biggest challenges in making a transition to a new economic class is maintaining relationships. Consider the following true story.

In New Orleans I met a young woman working as a secretary who had come from old money—until her family lost everything. Her father had been a partner in a law firm and, after his investments failed, started embezzling. He got caught and was disbarred but didn't go to prison. However, they went from living in a 15,000-square-foot home to a 1,500-square-foot apartment. The electricity got cut off at least once a month. But they kept their maid. It wasn't for social pretense, as you might suspect, that they kept their maid. Actually, their old friends didn't see them anymore. No, they kept her because there was so much they had never learned how to do. And it wasn't because their old friends didn't care about them that they weren't in contact. In fact, their old friends didn't call on them because they didn't want to embarrass them. As the young woman and her parents now had little discretionary cash to spend, it would have put them in awkward situations.

How much discretionary income do you go through in a week if you have a million dollars or more of income? Not the week you went to Australia for the Olympics. I'm talking about an ordinary week that you stay in town—the cash spent on golf games, beauty parlors, art openings, going out to eat, private clubs, and so forth.

Depending on where you live, that amount is between $1,500 and $2,000.

How much discretionary income do you spend in a week if you're in middle class? Somewhere between $50 and $150 per week, depending on your age.

If you wish to maintain your relationships with people who have remained middle class, you must remember that they don't have the same financial resources as you do, so you'll either have to do middle-class activities or treat them to mutual experiences. While you can now help the people you care about, this can pose difficulties too, as you may wonder on occasion if you're being taken advantage of or if your generosity is affecting the relationship. You may confront resentment and envy from people in your own family. Or you may just begin to feel as though everyone wants a "piece" of you.

Wealth comes with accountability to the people you hire and to the government, as well as your immediate family and relatives. You will need to work with a financial planner who can help you clarify your intentions and meet those goals. You must do whatever you need to do to educate yourself to handle your business affairs and assets. And if it seems beneficial and feels right to maintain relationships, you may have to be flexible and bend to the economic level of the people you love and value. You must make up your own mind whether or not to offer assistance to certain individuals so they can strive to improve their own circumstances. Not everyone will develop the ability to do so. But it's a journey made more possible with a greater number of resources, including role models and relationships, education, support systems, and (yes) access to money.

Learn the Hidden Rules

It can take more than a decade of juggling relationships, assets, and time frames to attain a degree of stability in the culture of new money. Many people make a smooth transition. Others feel the transition poses challenges they must struggle to overcome. If you're making the transition from middle class to new money and wealth, several misconceptions that exist in middle class will need to be addressed.

- You will pay taxes. After $250,000, you will lose most of your deductions. Although you can defer taxes, you will pay them eventually.

- Having money doesn't guarantee that you'll find good service. It takes trial and error. The best source is recommendations. Finding the connections that can give you the recommendations is like being in an unfamiliar room at night and still somehow finding the light switch.

- If you're new money, you do *not* get access to the *best* unless you're fortunate. For example, the best pieces of art are usually only available to new money through auctions. The best is reserved for those with the connections and longstanding relationships.

- Just because you have entrée into certain clubs, a resort, and so on doesn't mean you can meet the individuals you want to meet. And remember, don't introduce yourself at a social event; wait to be introduced.

- If you have good taste, you can select your own clothing. You'll be better off, though, if you find an excellent tailor and a personal shopping assistant. You will need both.

- At some point in the transition from middle class to wealth, time becomes more important than money. Quality becomes more important than quantity. Quantity carries with it the liabilities of storage, insurance, maintenance, and so forth. Why incur those costs for things that have little value? Consequently, fewer items of greater quality become more important.

- Privacy is no longer possible. In fact, it's a joke. You protect yourself as much as possible. However, your accountant, your trust lawyer, your corporate lawyer, your business manager, your investment counselor, your housekeepers, and others know more about particular aspects of your business affairs than you do. They have credit-card numbers, copies of your tax statements, and copies of your investments and other documents. Members of your households have access to the security systems, the locations of valuables, and so on. Those individuals who are most discreet are soon very well-compensated.

- Just because someone has expertise doesn't mean he/she has integrity.

- You can no longer say what you think. Almost everything you say is "amplified," dissected, and often misquoted.

- You will guard what you tell friends and family of origin about purchases, costs, and so forth. It often isn't understood.

- You must understand that golf plays a key role in the world of wealth. If invited to join an executive for golf, do not respond as one middle-class person did: "Who has time to chase a little white ball around?" Instead, enlist the services of a golf professional and take lessons, then spend some time practicing at the driving range and putting green.

- Humor and jokes tend to be about social *faux pas*.

- Some social invitations are accepted simply out of necessity.

- Social protocol is still observed in wealth—that is, who sits by whom, who is introduced first, who is deferred to in order of speaking, who makes the introductions. All individuals are *not* created equal in wealth.

▓ The weapon of choice in wealth is social exclusion. You simply will not be invited again.

Draw Upon Your Resources

One of the great privileges of wealth is the access it allows to human resources, such as expert teachers and professional assistance. If you need to host a networking party, for instance, you can hire a caterer and event coordinator to ensure its success. If you want to learn to play golf or tennis, you can hire an instructor. Your financial assets enable you to be entrepreneurial and take selected risks that a person from middle class couldn't afford to take. Generally, every issue that arises during the transition has a solution that someone has already devised, so you can draw upon his/her skills and knowledge. Even though you may find yourself in unfamiliar territory for a while, trust that you will become more confident and adept.

The same advice about seeking role models that applied to the transition from poverty to middle class (see Chapter 14) applies to the transition from middle class to wealth. There's a reason your transition is occurring; perhaps you and/or your spouse have enjoyed professional success, or perhaps you've married someone from money. If the transition originated in business, you may already have access to a career mentor who would be willing to share observations on the social sphere as well. A mentor who is willing to foster you in society is golden. If the transition originates from marriage, your best role models may be new family members. Seek out ways to strengthen your warm connections. Invite them to spend time with you; ask them to indulge your curiosity.

You and your partner are recognized as a team in the wealthy world. Love each other and show mutual support. Be honest about your challenges and help each other find the most appropriate solutions. Our partners are often the best resources we have.

CHAPTER 16

Communicating with Your Partner

A few summers ago in Texas it was so hot that the railroad tracks in the Fort Worth area warped. We keep butter out in our house, and the butter kept melting. One afternoon I was complaining to my husband, who was a science major in college, "This is ridiculous! It says 72 degrees on our thermostat, and the butter is melting. Yet, in the winter when it says 72 degrees, the butter doesn't melt." It was a problem that perplexed me.

Frank told me, "Ruby, never confuse real heat with measured heat. It is not the same thing." Boy, that was a news flash. Mr. Celsius and Mr. Fahrenheit were two scientists who wanted a better way to talk about heat than "It's so hot it warped the railroad tracks," so they developed an abstract system. But we must never forget that their system is an overlay on sensory-based reality. It is not the same thing.

Interestingly, the three economic classes in the United States learn to handle language differently. To survive in poverty, you must be sensory-based and nonverbal. You have to be able to remain alert and respond quickly for protection. To survive in middle class and in wealth, you need to be verbal and abstract. If you're middle class, you're concerned with work. You have a formal education. As we saw in Chapter 11, to work on paper and on the computer, you must understand how to represent tangibles by way of *in*tangible concepts (abstractions). You must be able to build structures inside your head that replicate external reality. If you're wealthy, those abstract structures may be even more complex. You perceive the world as a web of connections that span families, generations, organizations, and nations.

As you might imagine, the way people use language to express their everyday thoughts and feelings—and handle their differences—can have an enormous impact on their most intimate relationships, as well as on their job opportunities, their financial and legal matters, or the way they interact with authority figures. So let's explore communication.

Effective Communication

In 1967 a linguist named Martin Joos found that no matter what language is being spoken worldwide, there are five registers. The first register is known as *frozen.* Its words are always the same, like the Lord's Prayer, the Pledge of Allegiance, or wedding vows. The second register is *formal,* the type of language we use at work and in school. Formal register is often used in writing. The third is *consultative,* which tends to be a mix of formal and casual. Then, there's *casual,* the type of language that's used between friends. It comes out of the oral-language tradition of any group of people. Finally, we have *intimate* register. This is what's used between lovers and twins.

Joos found that when you go up or down one register in conversation it is socially acceptable. But if you go up or down two registers or more, people tend to be offended. For example, if you go to a wedding and a sermon is given after the vows, this would be OK because the speech is shifting from frozen to formal register. But if the minister, priest, or rabbi then turns to the audience and says, "Tell me about your own marriage. How's it going?" people would say, "That's incredibly tacky!" It would shock them.

In *Meaningful Differences in the Everyday Experience of Young American Children* (see Bibliography), Betty Hart and Todd R. Risley researched households by economic level and studied the amount of language children heard between the ages of one and three. They found that in welfare households children heard about 10 million words. They got one positive comment for every two negatives.

Positives would be phrases like "That's good" or "That's fine." Negatives would be "Don't do that" or "Stop that." In the working class, kids heard about 20 million words in those two years. They got two strokes for every discount. In professional households, children heard 30 million words in that same amount of time. They also got five positives for every negative. Regrettably, this research shows that a three-year-old in a professional household has more vocabulary than an adult in a welfare household.

One time I heard a husband and wife in Frank's neighborhood arguing for 15 minutes about who loved the cat most. But do you know what they were really arguing about? They were debating which of them was the most lovable. The trouble was: Because they were arguing at the personal level, they weren't making any headway.

In generational poverty, virtually the only language register people know is casual register. Unfortunately, to resolve a conflict, you have to get away from the level of the personal and go to the level of the issue. To operate on the level of issues, you have to be able to use abstract words. One of the reasons there's so much violence in poverty is that most people have only casual register. They simply don't have the words to resolve conflicts through conversation and discussion.

Conflict resolution will be addressed in the next chapter. Suffice it to say here, if you're in a relationship where one partner comes from a lower-income background and the other partner comes from middle class, you need to be prepared for some of your arguments to degenerate into the personal. These types of personal arguments are often over stuff that has to do with hidden rules. Even a college-educated person who knows formal register can get angry or emotional and revert to familiar (casual register) speech patterns. Middle-class and affluent people sometimes also say harsh words they don't mean.

Discourse is the meat, the logic, the reasoning of an argument. In formal register, we want people to get to the point. That's a middle-class way of thinking and speaking.

In casual register, you beat around the bush for a while before you get to the point. In Frank's old neighborhood, people throw in comments when someone is telling a story. The kinds of comments depend on the story, but they might include: "Talk to the hand, the elbow is not listening," or, "Well, she should have slapped him." Gestures also are used. When you're a really good storyteller, you can take the comments that are thrown at you and weave them into the story.

Since human beings can't communicate telepathically, if I were to ask you, "How far is it from Atlanta to Birmingham?" and you answered, "It's a far piece," it wouldn't help me much. But if you gave me an answer in miles or in units of time, there would be a shared understanding between us, and I could relate to the information.

To communicate effectively we need to have a shared understanding of a mental model, such as the length of a mile or the duration of an hour. Models are how we carry information. Usually the model is a story, an analogy, or a two-dimensional drawing. The model also tells you what is or is not important to the communicator. Hidden rules are abstract mental models. In your relationship, knowing the hidden rules of class can make a significant difference in how well you understand and communicate with each other.

Three Typical Scenarios

You and your husband are fighting. You tell your 12-year-old son that he must choose sides in this fight. If he agrees with his father, he's "no good—just like your daddy." If he does that, you threaten, you won't claim him as your son. Furthermore, you tell your sister about what your husband did. Your sister tells your brother-in-law that he'd better not talk to your husband again!

You and your spouse are fighting. You agree to some time to "cool off" before you continue the discussion. Both of you realize there are options that haven't been considered. When you argue, you try to do so where the children won't hear you. You don't want them to feel caught in the middle of the argument. You understand that your conflict with your spouse doesn't extend to the children.

You and your spouse are fighting. You agree that you will need to get legal and financial advice before you can make a decision. Your children are in boarding school and don't know about your argument. You're more concerned about the domestic staff. You don't want them to share the information with other domestic staffs, and you know that happens. In fact, that's often how you know what's going on in other households.

The Role of Polarized Thought

Polarized thinking is the yes/no, cut-and-dried approach. You're either for me or against me. A situation is black or white. There are no gray areas. Polarized thinking means that you have difficulty examining options and looking at choices. Examining options means you have the ability to look at a problem from an issue standpoint rather than a personal one. To do so requires abstract language and constructs.

The ability to make choices frees us. When people are processing on the body level mostly, they act on their feelings. They're impulsive. In other words: If you make me mad, I hit you. When you get to a metacognitive level, you represent feelings in the abstract. You have the ability to use words and phrases to describe them. You can say, "This incident made me angry" or, "I felt like David in front of Goliath."

If you've ever been so angry that you spent 45 minutes in the shower berating someone who wasn't there, you were making emotional deals. You were looking at the abstract ideas, or constructs, that made an incident happen—and when you found another way to think about it, that freed you. It is a quality-of-life issue. It gives you choices.

In poverty, abstract words and constructs often aren't learned. According to research, most individuals whose families have been in poverty two generations or more have a working conversational vocabulary of about 400 to 800 words. In professional households (meaning there's some education beyond high school), the commonly used speaking vocabulary is more in the range of 1,200 to

1,600 words, though other studies show that most college-educated professionals are familiar with the meanings of more than 40,000 words. Many of the additional words available in professional households are abstract words—that is, ideas, concepts, and "blueprints."

In *Your* Life . . .

Along with class issues and the ability to communicate, it should be noted that the levels of education of both members of a couple, their personalities, and their past history of relationships also have an effect on their reactions and interactions.

If you're from poverty and moving into middle class, understand that arguments and even insults usually will be given from an issue level. For example, the preference would be to phrase an insult in this way. Rather than say that a woman dresses like a whore, the comment would be: "It's such a shame that she doesn't know how to dress." Such a statement implies that the way of dressing comes out of a lack of intelligence instead of personal preference. In addition, options are examined, especially as they affect finances and work.

If you're from middle class and marry into poverty, expect that arguments will unexpectedly become personal because abstract frames of reference may not be available. Try to rephrase the argument as an issue and take it away from the personal.

The hardest thing about reframing an issue is figuring out a way to do it that will make sense to the individual with whom you're speaking. People tend to avoid doing or accepting anything that conflicts with who they are. When you're reframing for another person, you're trying to find a way they can engage in a behavior that won't be in conflict with their identity.

If you're from middle class and marry into wealth, understand that options will almost always be examined—particularly from legal, political, and social perspectives. Further, experts will be involved in the determination of issues. Expect that arguments will occur over artistic merit, expertise, and *details*. I heard of a wealthy industrialist couple that, while traveling abroad, argued at length over how many bathrooms they had in their house back in Manitoba. He said seven; she said six. Because accounting, law, and aesthetic factors allow for individual interpretations, arguments will revolve around those issues. Rarely will the discussion be about polarities.

A helpful technique for anyone who wants to help a spouse learn a new abstract concept is to help that person identify the stimulus (the what), give it meaning (the why), and then offer an intervention (the how). This is like saying to a young child, "Don't cross the street without looking." That's *what* we want them to pay attention to. *Why?* "You could be killed." That's the meaning. *How:* "Look both ways twice."

Remember, it makes a significant difference in learning if a caring person, such as you, explains the hidden rules. Our relationships motivate us to learn and evolve.

Child, Parent, and Adult Voices

Dr. Eric Berne, the founder of Transactional Analysis, describes the human personality as composed of three "ego states" (Child, Parent, and Adult) that represent specific mindsets and have different types of interactions with the world. He calls their communication styles "transactions." Have you ever noticed that the voice in your head sometimes whines, begs, resists, or expresses delight? That is the Child voice. When you're in the Parent voice, you're being firm and insistent, but a negative Parent voice is when your index finger goes up and you start uttering words like *should* or *ought*. When you're using the Adult voice, you're asking questions, you're direct, and you're calm.

Most of us go into the negative Parent voice when a belief of some kind gets triggered. Those beliefs are our personal hidden rules of conduct, which may relate to class or something else. Then we come up with a "should" or "ought" message. I'll use a story about myself to illustrate how this works, though I'm not proud of it.

I was in the airport. I had two or three more hours of flying to go, and I was tired. It was about 9 p.m. My stuff went through security (a box of books, a suitcase, and so on), and one of the guards, a girl who was maybe 18, pointed to the box of books and asked me, "What's in here?"

I said, "Look, it holds books. It has never been opened. It's labeled." I didn't want to open it, because then I would've had to find tape to reseal it. It would be a mess.

In her parent voice, she said to me, "OPEN IT."

Well, the little voice in my head started up with its "shoulds" and "oughts." It sounded something like this: "You're older than she is. She *should* be polite to you." So I responded, "Pardon me?"

She looked at me, and she said, "I SAID, OPEN IT."

The voice in my head got louder and faster, and I said to her, "You don't have 'please' or 'thank you' in your vocabulary?"

As you can imagine, she didn't like that much. She looked at me and said, "*I DON'T HAVE TO SAY PLEASE OR THANK YOU TO YOU!*"

Well, I just lost it. "*YOU DO TOO!*" Oh, it was awful. The line behind me got horribly backed up. People were gawking. I got in her face. She got in mine. The manager came over. In the end, though I didn't have to open the box, I did spend 20 minutes stuck in security.

It's human nature when someone approaches you with that insistent parental voice to resist it. *You wanta bet?* we all think. So when you hear that voice coming from your partner's mouth, you may be able to avoid a head-on collision if you can remain calm and be selective about your responses.

Here are a few rules of thumb for conversing with your partner:

- Be direct and use a calm, appropriate voice. You are speaking to an equal.

- If you want to change a behavior, make a request using the Adult voice. Otherwise, your partner is likely to respond as a Parent or as a Child.

- If you're feeling emotional, take a deep breath to keep the oxygen flowing to your brain. This will help keep you alert and relaxed.

- When you are the listener, occasionally paraphrase back to your partner what your partner is saying to you. This way your partner knows you're listening and can correct any misstatements or misrepresentations that have crept into the conversation.

- Be quiet when your partner is speaking. Allow him/her to finish before jumping in and responding.

- Probe for details. These are: who, what, where, why, and when.

- Speak in the "I" voice, from your own experience. Avoid blaming, "You this . . . You that . . ."

- A strategy for people who don't have formal register storytelling ability is to ask them to tell a story three times. The first time, they tell it and you listen. The second time, they tell it and you interrupt to ask questions. The third time, you tell it back to them and they stop you to fill in the gaps and correct your mistakes.

- Admit "I don't know" when you don't know.

CHAPTER 17

Managing and Resolving Your Conflicts

*W*ere you originally surprised to discover that the person you're dating or chose to marry interprets the world and makes decisions based on an entirely different set of assumptions than yours? While it's common sense that someone from a different class background would not be the same, if you were like most people, at first you probably didn't realize how pronounced and pervasive such differences would be. As you've seen throughout this book, there are hidden rules of class for a broad range of issues, including money, gender, appearance, social activities, children, education, work, home maintenance, and religion. In other words, even in the most genuinely loving relationships between partners who are committed to harmony, there are plenty of opportunities for disagreement. It's true what someone once said about human variety and diversity: "People don't just *pretend* to be different, they really *are*."

Conflict is completely natural, and it comes with the territory in relationships. Research has shown there are different stages in marriage. During the first one or two years, a couple may be in a state of bliss and romantic infatuation. Then, for the next decade or so, the marriage will incorporate a process of negotiation. According to John Bradshaw, this period is when family-of-origin issues, such as economic class differences, come into play. In *Healing the Shame That Binds You* (see Bibliography), he writes: "The journey toward intimacy is marked by the following: healthy conflict, learning to negotiate and fight fair, patience, hard work, and the courage to risk being an individual. Above all it is marked by a willingness to embrace a disciplined love."

There are several distinct philosophies about conflict. Some people believe it's undesirable and should be eliminated. Others believe it's a normal aspect of relating, but not particularly wanted. Still others believe conflict is absolutely necessary because it stimulates curiosity and change. Obviously, conflict can be both useful and destructive. Part of the reason people enjoy marriage, in addition to the companionship it provides, is that it helps them clarify their values and assess their capabilities. United, couples are stronger than they are alone. Although choosing to respect and honor each other's individuality isn't always easy — people are very different — it's worth it.

In this final chapter, let's look at some ways you might manage your conflicts. Many of these are strategies that I learned from my work as a principal and from research done for a doctorate on conflict resolution by principals in the school setting. They can be applied, however, to one-on-one relationships as well. Other techniques are drawn from interviews with individuals whose spouse grew up in a different economic class.

What Are the Sources of Conflict?

If you and your significant other have shared priorities, goals, and beliefs, conflict and stress will be minimized. *Webster's* defines stress as "struggle resulting from incompatible or opposing needs, drives, wishes, or external or internal demands." In a marriage, stress factors, or points of conflict, might include:

- Personal need for closeness or distance.

- Difficulties coping with in-laws.

- Requirements of a business or a hobby.

- Challenges of childrearing.

▪ Illness.

▪ Communication.

▪ Time management.

▪ Finances.

▪ Decision making.

▪ Planning and organizational skills.

Hidden rules of class can underlie issues in each of these categories.

A middle-class woman describes a conflict in her marriage to a man who grew up in the culture of poverty.

> *I come from a family of big planners, so that's what I learned and brought into the marriage. We're 30 years married and, to this day, he's not a time person, whereas I sit down and plan my day backward. He has no clue of how to do that. Yes, he meets deadlines on the job, but he goes about his life a different way. He has fun.*
>
> *Every time we go somewhere, his lack of time planning is a source of tension. If we agree to leave at 12 o'clock, that's when he really starts getting ready. He puts his shoes on then. It drives me crazy, but I just sit and wait and accept it and go on. I like to choose my battles. He goes at a slow, easygoing pace, and I'm fighting it all day long.*
>
> *Although this is a personality trait, his family does the same thing. To this day, when his parents come see us (they're old now) they never tell us the day they'll arrive or the day they'll leave. Heck, I never knew they were coming. It nearly drove me insane. One time I packed my bag!*

A wife from poverty describes a source of conflict in her marriage to a middle-class man: "My husband's tight with his money. He wants to save. I want to spend. When he was going to retire, I was like,

'Great! Now we can finally spend some of our money.' Why not? He said, 'We might move out into the street next week.' I asked him, 'Honey, we've worked hard, and now we're just supposed to die and leave it all to our son, who'll spend it in 15 minutes?' We had to reach a compromise."

From our exploration of the hidden rules of class in earlier chapters, the tendencies of both husbands are recognizable as specific mindsets.

Often it's a spouse's response to the other's different mindset or behavior that dictates whether tension ultimately arises. "The gift of dialogue: That's my strength, because he doesn't talk," says a third woman who feels she has been able to sidestep many conflicts with her husband raised in poverty. "It has gotten better. At the beginning, I would ask questions and pry and probe, and sometimes that worked in my favor and sometimes not. I might want to talk and he said, 'No,' and then I had to wait. I believe one of the things that can keep you on an even keel in marriage is the ability to dialogue."

Recently, I had a conversation with an African-American gentleman who is a resident of Shaker Heights, the most affluent suburb of Cleveland. Both the very poor and the very wealthy live in his area. He told me, "You don't know how freeing it was to hear about the hidden rules. I'd always thought that the issues in our community were about race. Now I know that they're as much about money as anything else." I took this as another confirmation that understanding the hidden rules of class is liberating.

In my experience, when a hidden rule is not articulated, you and your significant other think you're arguing about a personal matter, something unique to your experience with each other. The research on conflict resolution says you can't resolve a conflict unless you go to the issue level. As long as you stay at the personal level, you're not likely to make much progress. The specifics may change, yet the rule will haunt you. Many difficult issues become workable once you agree upon the nature of the issues.

The Daily Dance and Negotiation: Win/Lose vs. Win/Win

Mindsets of win/win or win/lose make a considerable difference in the outcome of personal disputes. In a win/lose scenario, people can get hurt—sometimes badly. Experts have identified five styles of conflict resolution. You'll notice that each represents a combination of some degree of assertion or passivity and some degree of cooperation or lack of cooperation. Cooperative approaches are aimed at win/win solutions. By contrast, uncooperative approaches are targeted to win/lose outcomes. The five styles are:

1. **Competing:** Assertive and uncooperative. This is a power-oriented mode in which a partner pursues his/her own concerns at the other's expense and uses whatever power seems necessary to win, such as the ability to argue, a rank, economic sanctions, and so forth.

2. **Accommodating:** Unassertive and cooperative. This is the opposite of competing. In this mode, a partner neglects his/her own concerns to satisfy the concerns of the other. It has an element of self-sacrifice. Accommodating might take the form of selfless generosity or charity, obeying a spouse's order when you would prefer not to, or yielding to a spouse's point of view.

3. **Avoiding:** Passive and uncooperative. In this mode, a partner doesn't immediately pursue his/her own concerns or those of the other. He/she doesn't address the conflict. Avoiding might take the form of diplomatically sidestepping an issue altogether, postponing an issue until a better time, or simply withdrawing from a threatening situation.

4. **Compromising:** Intermediate levels of assertion and cooperation. The objective is to find an expedient, mutually acceptable solution that *partially* satisfies *both* partners.

Compromising falls in the middle ground between competing and accommodating. This mode gives up more than competing and less than accommodating. Likewise, it explores an issue more directly than avoiding, but doesn't explore it in as much depth as collaborating. It might mean splitting the difference, exchanging concessions, *quid quo pro* ("you scratch my back and I'll scratch yours"), or seeking a quick middle position.

5. **Collaborating:** Assertive and cooperative. This is the opposite of avoiding. Collaborating involves a partner's attempt to work with the other to find some solution that *fully* satisfies the concerns of *both* persons. It means digging into an issue to identify the underlying concerns of the two individuals and to find an alternative that meets both sets of concerns. Collaborating between spouses might take the form of exploring a disagreement to learn from each other's insights, deciding to rectify circumstances that would otherwise have them competing, or confronting an interpersonal problem and seeking to find a creative solution.

There are three essential ingredients in effective conflict resolution.

- You must have a personal commitment to resolving the problem that you and your spouse are facing.

- Both parties must have a common interest in resolving the problem.

- There must be communication. You and your spouse must each take responsibility for your contribution on all of these levels. Otherwise it won't happen.

In *The Seven Habits of Highly Effective People* (see Bibliography), Stephen Covey indicates that building and repairing relationships is a long-term investment. He suggests six ways to do so:

1. Understanding the individual.

2. Attending to the little things.

3. Keeping commitments.

4. Clarifying expectations.

5. Showing personal integrity.

6. Apologizing sincerely when a mistake is made.

There have been many studies of teamwork in organizations, and it seems as though many of these same principles would work in marital relationships. One of the most important characteristics is being able to communicate and listen, not only to what is said, but also to what is not said. The difference between great teams and mediocre teams lies in their approach to conflict and to dealing with the defensiveness that invariably surrounds conflict. Mediocre teams are unable to listen "between the lines."

In her book *You Just Don't Understand* (see Bibliography) on the different communication styles of men and women, Deborah Tannen says, "The biggest mistake is believing there is one right way to listen, to talk, to have a conversation—or a relationship. Nothing hurts more than being told your intentions are bad when you know they are good, or being told you are doing something wrong when you know you're just doing it your way." This insight applies as much to relationships and conversation between spouses from different classes as it does to men and women in general. Everyone's way of working at it makes sense in a familiar context.

Questionnaire: How Do You Handle Conflicts?

The following questions are designed to lead you through a mutual process of self-evaluation and discovery. They cannot be answered with a simple yes or no. You may choose to use these questions as the basis of a conversation with your significant other. Or you may prefer to mull them over in privacy. My hope is that they will stir up insights regarding the personal resources you draw upon, or could draw upon in the future, when you are confronting a disagreement, or other type of clash, with your partner.

Remember, ten qualities of resilient relationships are: integrity, financial resources, emotional resources, mental resources, spiritual resources, physical resources, support systems, relationships and role models, knowledge of hidden rules, and desire and persistence. You can review these by rereading Chapter 2.

1. What aspects of your situation create the most conflicts for you?

2. Of those conflicts, which seem most stressful to you?

3. What actions do you take in these situations that contribute to your success?

4. What specific abilities do you bring to these situations that promote success?

5. When you and your significant other are involved in a conflict, how often do you rely upon or ask others to help you resolve the conflict?

6. How often would you be able to resolve the conflict without their help?

7. What kinds of stressful or conflict-producing situations do you avoid?

8. When you avoid a conflict or a stressful situation, how does it get resolved?

9. In what ways do you handle conflict differently now than when you began the relationship?

10. How often in a situation of conflict or stress do you feel that the success of the outcome depended upon factors outside of yourself?

Make Up Your Own Rules

By now it's probably apparent that every couple has to reach their own agreement about how to live, as well as which set or sets of hidden rules of class to follow—and when. You and your spouse/partner have the opportunity to be as true to your own values and beliefs as the individuals and couples in this book who have shared their relationship stories.

Among other things, it's vital to be gentle with our partners, as we don't want to push their emotional buttons. Let's listen to a woman who grew up in extreme poverty.

> One sticking point with my husband, on my part, has been that whenever he disagreed with me about something I'd done, like spending too much money or forgetting to document a transaction—those kinds of things—I would get upset. I've come to realize that it takes me back to when I was at home as a young girl and always criticized. Thus, I had a hard time accepting correction or disagreement and saw it all as criticism. That was hard for him. He didn't know where it came from.
>
> Because of my childhood, I didn't know how to negotiate. I didn't have a large vocabulary. So I'd just get mad, blow up, refuse to talk, or repeat myself. I needed to do something about my reaction. I'm better about it than when I was younger, and I understand its origins, whereas I didn't before. But even now, if I don't do positive self-talk, I can still go back into those emotional areas.

Here are some of the strategies that others have devised, in their own words:

- "We try not to go to bed angry. But one time I kept flipping on the light, and my wife finally said, 'Go to bed, Honey, for gosh sakes.' "

- "We have a rule when we're arguing because we're very much alike: If you're mad at me today, I can't be mad at you. Because when two people get mad and start fighting, you don't get anything resolved."

■ "One of the things we decided on early was that we'd never quit anything on the same day. Not a job or anything."

■ "We never make a purchase over $100 without leaving the store, talking about it, and making the purchase later. That is our rule: Never buy on the spot. He follows through with that even now that we don't have to be as careful. He e-mailed me a picture of a dining room table before buying, even though we'd orally agreed."

■ "Time heals so much. I give him space and time. We may not talk a whole lot. I can't totally clam up; it's not me. So we talk, but I get quieter. He'll come around."

■ "Let stuff go. The smallest thing, if you keep at it, will turn into more than it was to begin with."

■ "Choose your battles. A lot of things aren't open for discussion—that's the way it is."

■ "We avoid her parents. Our marriage would never have lasted if we'd been around them a lot. I couldn't have handled it."

■ "We take turns supporting each other. We handle stress differently. He naps or goes to the movies. I talk to a friend. We each have coping strategies."

■ "Focus on the day right ahead of you. But keep planning to get better. Ask: How can I make this work? Make it work. You're not looking too far ahead, and you're not so absorbed that there's no tomorrow. You can't stay exactly in the moment, because you might get left behind, so you have to juggle."

- ■ "I needed to be empathetic to her feelings, rather than tell her she can't feel a certain way. Why I originally sometimes said no was simply because I was being insensitive to her feelings. I thought I knew everything. But I don't know. I wasn't sensitive. I find that if we listen to people instead of always trying to come back with something, they can teach us."

- ■ "Be verbally appreciative. That makes such a difference!"

- ■ "My husband and I are good at communicating. We can have a 'knock-down-drag-out' with our voices lowered. We argue a little, but I usually give in and go on. Some things don't matter. If you can see the good at the end, that's what matters."

Love Is the Common Ground

Relationships and marriage are wonderful at times, hard work at times. Yet the human desire for love and belonging is a real and powerful force in our lives. We may occasionally argue with our mate; we may often be perplexed by the way he/she thinks or behaves. But there was something that drew us together at the beginning, and it *is* possible to harness this attraction to solidify our connection. Love is always our common ground.

Understanding and acceptance are not contingent on similarity. It doesn't matter if you believe that opposites attract or repel. If you come from dissimilar backgrounds, that's simply the environment you and your spouse inhabit. Wishing this were not so is to deny reality. When you look into your partner's eyes, you are privileged to be seeing an entire world of unique experience and feeling and insight. Not everyone receives this opportunity. It is special, valuable, and worth preserving.

Thankfully, we have the option to approach each other with mutual respect and conscious commitment. For better and for worse, our partnerships transcend us and enhance us. In the real world, how do we cope with our differences—whatever they may be? Well, every day we can choose to honor our partner's truth and perspective, and we can request that our partner honors ours. Our mutual expectations can—and perhaps should—be high, so that we don't end up settling for less than the best. Those expectations are like the North Star leading us past incidental obstacles, reminding us to seek what is good.

Throughout this book, you have read about typical patterns of mindsets and behavior from the different classes. These hidden rules are some of the underlying principles by which people guide their lives, including you and me, your significant other, and our friends, family members, and co-workers. In the darkness of night, these hidden rules may seem dangerous. Bringing them into the sunlight, we see them for what they are: survival strategies and embellishments of group culture. They are the stuff of life—and not necessarily harmful nor shameful. We're all just different folks doing our best to get by in the world. That's not so hard to love, understand, and accept, is it?

I hope this information proves as helpful to you in your life as it has in mine. Blessings to you on the journey.

Bibliography

Berne, Eric. (1986). *Transactional Analysis in Psychotherapy.* New York, NY: Ballantine.

Bradshaw, John. (1988). *Healing the Shame That Binds You.* Deerfield Beach, FL: Health Communications.

Covey, Stephen. (1989). *The Seven Habits of Highly Effective People.* New York, NY: Simon & Schuster.

Graham, Lawrence Otis. (1999). *Our Kind of People.* New York, NY: HarperCollins.

Greenspan, Stanley I. (1998). *The Growth of the Mind.* New York, NY: Perseus.

Hart, Betty, & Risley, Todd R. (1995). *Meaningful Differences in the Everyday Experience of Young American Children.* Baltimore, MD: Paul H. Brookes.

Joos, Martin. (1967). The styles of the five clocks. *Language and Cultural Diversity in American Education.* (1972). Abrahams, R.D., & Troike, R.C. (Eds.). Englewood Cliffs, NJ: Prentice-Hall.

Koenig, Harold G. (1999). *The Healing Power of Faith.* New York, NY: Simon & Schuster.

Krabill, Don L., & Payne, Ruby K. (2002). *Hidden Rules of Class at Work.* Highlands, TX: aha! Process.

Molloy, John T. (1996). *New Women's Dress for Success.* New York, NY: Warner.

Molloy, John T. (1988). *John T. Molloy's New Dress for Success.* New York, NY: Warner.

Payne, Ruby K., DeVol, Philip, & Smith, Terie Dreussi. (2001). *Bridges Out of Poverty.* Highlands, TX: aha! Process.

Payne, Ruby K. (2003). *A Framework for Understanding Poverty* (Third Revised Edition). Highlands, TX: aha! Process.

Payne, Ruby K. (2002). *Understanding Learning.* Highlands, TX: aha! Process.

Payne, Ruby K. (1994). A study of the relationships among stress resiliency indicators and conflict management styles of school principals. Doctoral dissertation. Chicago, IL: Loyola University.

Smith, Stuart C., & Huffstutter, Sandra. (1989). Managing time and stress. *School Leadership* (Second Edition). University of Oregon. Eugene, OR: ERIC Clearinghouse on Educational Management.

Sommers, Bill, & Payne, Ruby K. (2001). *Living on a Tightrope.* Highlands, TX: aha! Process.

Tannen, Deborah. (1990). *You Just Don't Understand.* New York, NY: Ballantine.

About the Author

Dr. Ruby Payne's career-long mission is to positively impact the education and lives of people in poverty throughout the world. Since 1972, when she first took up the role of professional educator, success has followed her efforts. Initially a teacher and principal, later an educational consultant, she is now also a trainer, speaker, author, business owner, and publisher. In short, she has become the *go-to expert* on the effects of class differences on relationships, whether at home, at work, in organizations, or in educational settings.

Her own educational background includes a B.A. from Goshen College, an M.S. in English Literature from Western Michigan University, and a Ph.D. in Educational Leadership and Policy Studies from Loyola University.

Dynamic and accessible, Dr. Payne speaks at more than 180 engagements per year. Business and community leaders, educators, and social service workers all benefit from her practical and creative solutions to the challenges posed by socioeconomic differences between individuals.

A prolific author, Dr. Payne has written or co-authored more than a dozen books, including her seminal *A Framework for Understanding Poverty*, which has sold more than 800,000 copies since its release in 1996. For a complete catalogue of titles, please visit www.ahaprocess.com.

As founder and CEO of **aha!** Process, Inc., a highly successful publishing and training company, Dr. Payne oversees a cadre of more than 50 consultant presenters. She alone has certified more than 5,000 *Framework* trainers around the world. Her training programs include a dozen seminars on the subject of poverty and class differences, while her publishing credits number more than three dozen books and video products.

Like no one else, Ruby K. Payne, Ph.D., is at the forefront of understanding and action in the field of class differences and poverty. Her decades-long study of the "hidden rules" of class has brought eye-opening insight and practical solutions to thousands of people who, like her, desire to raise the level of understanding, communication, and cooperation between and among people of all classes.

To find out more about Dr. Payne, her published works, and her training programs, visit www.ahaprocess.com, or call (800) 424-9484 or (281) 426-5300.

Eye-openers at ...
www.ahaprocess.com

▦ Join our **aha!** news list

    Receive our free newsletter with periodic news, updates, recent articles by Dr. Ruby K. Payne, and more! And get a free book, *Understanding Learning*, when you join!

▦ Tell us how this information has impacted your life; submit your story at www.crossingthetracksforlove.com

▦ Register online for Dr. Payne's U.S. National Tour

▦ Visit our online store

    Books, videos, workshops

▦ Learn about our Training Certification programs

    A Framework for Understanding Poverty

    Bridges Out of Poverty

    Meeting Standards & Raising Test Scores

▦ Register for courses at our Training Center